Be Great!

Behind the Mask by Takeo Spikes

Contact information:
T. Spikes Publishing
3500 Lenox Road, Suite 575 Atlanta, GA 30326

For more information about Behind the Mask, including bulk sales, and special project opts please visit www.behindthemaskbook.com

Book Cover and Layout Design by DL Warfield for GOLDFINGER c.s
Written and edited by: Takeo Spikes and Michael B. Jordan
Photographers: Takeo Spikes and Michael Moreland

ISBN-13: 978-0-692-75898-4
ISBN-10:0-692-75898-4

LCCN: Cataloging-in-Publication Data has been applied for First Edition

Table *of* Contents

Dedication

I would like to dedicate this book to my late father, Jimmie L. Spikes and my mother, Lillie Spikes. My mother stressed the importance of education and told me, "you know you can't play football forever." You were right! While I no longer play football, I have fulfilled and achieved three personal goals, completing both my undergraduate and graduate degree and completing my legacy— *"Behind The Mask"* for that I honor you. My dad's humility, integrity, and perseverance in the way he lived his life showed my family the way a man is supposed to conduct himself regardless of the situation, and he left the blueprint for all of us to follow. And for that, I'm forever grateful to be raised by a man's man.

FOREWARD BY DICK LEBEAU

I sometimes think back to my youth, a young man growing up in a small Midwestern town – London, Ohio. Weather permitting, we were always outside playing, every day, every season. We would carefully set the 'KEEP OFF THE GRASS' signs down in the alley that ran beside the post office lawn. It was the only stretch of ground unencumbered enough to permit a good old game of tackle football. Sometimes it was the West End vs the East End, or the South End, or the North End, or anybody we could find to compete against.

The powers-that-be would gently look the other way as we relentlessly chopped up their freshly mown lawn. What great fun and healthy activity it was for us budding, would-be London high school varsity players.

Little did I realize that my adversaries from across the street would someday turn out to be the finest football players in the world, and it would be my honor to either play or coach against them for an entire lifetime.

I often think of all the great names of athletes that I have been fortunate enough to see and know and interact with at some level.

One of my favorite names that never fails to make an early appearance in my thoughts is Takeo Spikes, mostly because of his very unique talent, character, and personality, but even a little more so because he owns the somewhat dubious distinction of having played the most number of football games in the NFL without ever appearing in a playoff game.

I often refer to Takeo's unique challenge of competing on a daily basis, winning almost every individual award for excellence the game of football can bestow at every level and never having the opportunity to compete for the Lombardi Trophy.

That Takeo dealt with this throughout his distinguished 15-year career in the National Football League without ever having a mention or hint of disappointment is only further testimony to his great competitive character and leadership abilities.

Takeo means warrior, and never was a man more aptly named. We drafted him in the first round of the 1998 NFL Draft, and he immediately took us from nowhere to the eighth-best defense in the League. The next year, he was voted a team captain, an honor attained almost every one of his fifteen years.

Later, I had the privilege of coaching Takeo in Buffalo in the 2003 season, where he joined forces with London Fletcher at the linebacker position. Once again, the two men took us from nowhere to the second-rated defense in the NFL.

Takeo Spikes is a representative of all that is good in the National Football League. For fifteen years, he was one of the most outstanding players, teammates, citizens, and parents of the National Football League. I am proud to call him my friend. One of my most prized possessions is a picture of Takeo and I together on the sideline in the middle of a game discussing our next move. The picture carries a Father's Day date on it and is inscribed, 'To Pops, Happy Father's Day.' –Takeo.

I feel certain you will enjoy this book, put together by a linebacker, about linebackers. It is obviously a labor of love, created with the same passion and energy as he devoted to his All-Pro career. When you're talking about linebackers, Takeo Spikes is a very good place to start. Enjoy.

Dick LeBeau is in his 58th year in the NFL as a player or coach and his second with the Titans as Assistant Head Coach/ Defensive Coordinator. He was inducted into the NFL Hall of Fame in 2010.

NOTE FROM THE AUTHOR

Behind the Mask goes inside the mind of 12 NFL Hall of Fame caliber players with unique and intimate images and original, never-before-published content. The book profiles the greatest NFL linebackers of all time in a way that is deeper and more insightful than anything that has been published before. In *Behind the Mask*, the most sought after NFL players share with another elite-class football player what they only say to each other. Players have been carefully chosen to be the greatest names with the most unique stories on and off the field. The players' insights are focused on one topic: What made these players outliers? How did they achieve greatness that was well outside the norm?

Behind the Mask profiles linebackers because they are football's fiercest gridiron warriors. Linebackers are to the defense what the quarterback is to the offense: the on-field coach, the team leader, the heartbeat. Linebackers make impact plays every facet of a defensive call, stopping both runs and passes. Good linebackers require the trifecta of strength, speed, and smarts. But good linebackers are beyond talented; they feel the pulse of the game. They become the game.
The linebacker position is the most physically demanding position on an NFL team. They take great risk and physical hits from other players in their pursuit of the quarterback and ball carrier. The average career of an NFL player is three years. A linebacker who plays more than three years is very rare. The players profiled in this book are linebackers who played for 10 to 15 years, which makes them the rarest and toughest of all NFL players, including Mike Singletary, Derrick Brooks, Chuck Bednarik and Willie Lanier. The linebackers chosen for this book are linebackers who defined the position and raised the level of play. They are also players who were integral to championship wins for their teams, including the Chicago Bears, Oakland Raiders, and New York Giants.

Men and women who love the game are fascinated by the talent and personalities who played the game. You as a reader will learn what these players consider their secrets of greatness. You can use this knowledge to feed your passion and interest, as well as apply the wisdom to your own life.

Because of my 15-year NFL All Pro experience, the players granted me unprecedented access to photograph their private lives. Many of these athletes have not granted interviews in years. The players reveal to me their innermost thinking on what propelled them to seek excellence, how they achieved greatness, how they dealt with adversity, and how they grew through change on and off the field. These innermost thoughts are special and unique because it's what players only say to each other. And I'm sharing it with the world in Behind the Mask.

12

CHUCK BEDNARIK
NO.60

BORN: BETHLEHEM, PA

COLLEGE: PENNSYLVANIA STATE UNIVERSITY

NFL CAREER: 14 SEASONS

NFL TEAM: PHILADELPHIA EAGLES, 1949-1962

HALL OF FAME INDUCTION: 1967

CAREER HIGHLIGHTS AND AWARDS

8× PRO BOWL (1950–1956, 1960)

10× ALL-PRO (1950–1957, 1960, 1961)

2× NFL CHAMPION (1949, 1960)

PRO BOWL MVP (1953)

MAXWELL AWARD (1948)

NFL 50TH ANNIVERSARY ALL-TIME TEAM

NFL 75TH ANNIVERSARY ALL-TIME TEAM

NFL 1950S ALL-DECADE TEAM

EAGLES HALL OF FAME

PHILADELPHIA EAGLES #60 RETIRED

"Ďakujem. That means, 'Thank you.'"

There's an iconic image of the late Chuck Bednarik, which you can easily find on the internet. He's standing up on the field during a game, wearing his #60 Philadelphia Eagles jersey and drawing back a fist while looking down at a flattened, motionless player, with his head slightly cocked. Lying on his back near Bednarik's feet is Frank Gifford, at the time the NFL's most marketable player, pictured after a famous hit that would cause him to temporarily retire from the NFL for over a year.

It's by the image of this hit—and the countless times it was mentioned by Howard Cosell—that most people will remember Chuck Bednarik, who earned a place in Halls of Fame for both College and Pro Football, multiple Super Bowl rings and Pro Bowl appearances, the affection and gratitude of fans inside and outside Philadelphia, and the nickname Concrete Charlie. And it is one of the many reasons he wanted to express gratitude—in Slovak, the native language of his ancestors—to God, and the entire world, before he died.

Born in Bethlehem, Pennsylvania, to Slovakian immigrant parents who worked for Bethlehem Steel Mill, Bednarik was a child of the Great Depression, just under five years old when the market crashed. "I had a tough life coming up. The Depression came along as I was growing up, and it was terrible. We had to go to family welfare for clothes, for food. It was tough. As a kid growing up in Lehigh Valley, I used to go to watch basketball, wrestling, and all the sports; I'd climb the fence and sneak in ahead of time. When the Depression broke up, I went out for football and made it very easily, just from the fact that I loved the sport itself as a kid. I just picked it up and went along with it."

The reality of life in those formative years almost turned Bednarik, a naturally talented athlete, away from the game. Though he performed well playing for Liberty High School, he wasn't quite convinced that football was a path he should follow. His son-in-law, Ken Safarowic, remembers Bednarik telling stories of his life, including how he ended up on the path to his destiny. "The thing about players like Chuck is they were not touted with intentions of going to college. It was nowhere in the periphery. I don't think he ever envisioned greatness or it was predicted for him. Like so many guys from that era, coming out of World War II, football was nothing. He just played, and never expected to make a career out of it." His parents had lined up a job for him at the steel mill, but Liberty High School coach John Butler convinced him to look at other options. "He was a big impression," Bednarik says, remembering the conversation. "I said, 'College? That's not for me.' He said, 'Yes it is.' So I said, 'Okay, I'll give it a try.'" Safarowic remembers the story being a bit more colorful in tone. "Butler told him, 'You dumb Slovak; you're going to Penn State to play football for George Munger.'"

Safarowic spent a great deal of time with Bednarik before his passing and wrote a biography, *Concrete Charlie: An Oral History of Philadelphia's Greatest Football Legend Chuck Bednarik*, from research and conversational notes. He says that Bednarik's dedication to Catholicism was key to his life story. "God had something special planned for him, Safarowic says. "This is a man who went to church every day until he couldn't drive himself any more. He was as devoted a Catholic that you could find; he went to mass seven days a week. I really think somehow God said to him, 'If you give me your unwavering devotion, I will give you a historic, epic life. Maybe it had something to do that he was born in Bethlehem and mother's name was Mary. So many things that happened—silly, circumstantial things that make you think somebody up above had a plan and was guiding the plotline, because it was a combo of heaven by way of Hollywood."

In the midst of World War II, Bednarik ended up being drafted into the U.S. Army Air Force, to serve as a gunner on a B-24 bomber jet, while still in his senior year of high school. He started basic training before graduation—his mother even picked up his diploma for him. He flew 30 missions over Germany, in live combat. "Oh yeah, I was afraid of war. Planes were going down like crazy. I used to say my rosary every day a couple times. I carried rosary beads with me.

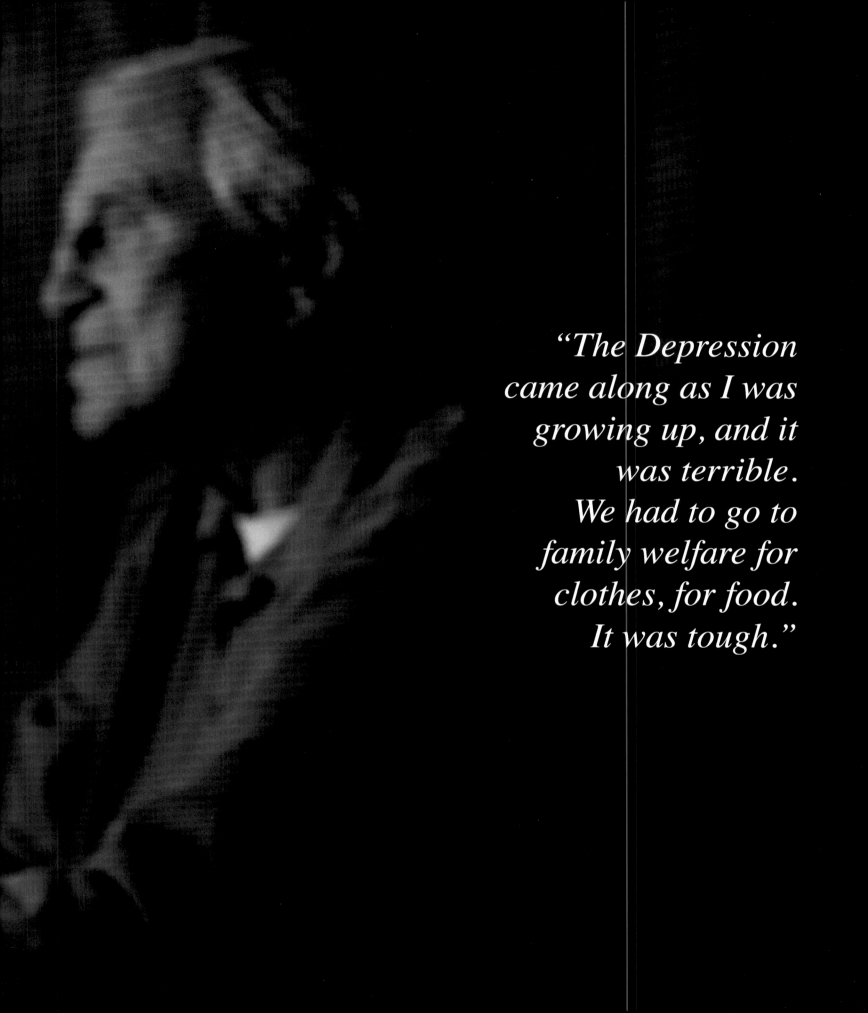

"The Depression came along as I was growing up, and it was terrible. We had to go to family welfare for clothes, for food. It was tough."

"When I'd get out of the plane, I'd take my rosary, kiss it, scrub the plane with it and say, 'Thank you.' Sometimes there'd be bullet holes in the plane. We crash-landed about four times. There was a lot of anti-aircraft missiles. It started soon as you hit France, the English Channel. Whew. I was lucky to come home alive. I remember the day we came back. I kissed the ground and looked up at God and said, 'Thank you.' And 'I don't ever want to fly again.'"

After serving, Bednarik attended the University of Pennsylvania. He joined the Quakers' football team in September, after the season had already started. "Guys he played with say they never saw anything like it," Safarowic says. "This kid from a steel town shows up and started, and is the biggest, strongest, fastest player they ever saw. He blocked, tackled, and threw the ball. He played center, but he could have played any position on the field and would have been a star anywhere."

Bednarik excelled. He would miss only three games in his 14 years as an Eagle, and his versatility kept him playing the whole time. He was a "sixty-minute man"—a two-way player who stayed on the field for the entire game, playing center on offense, defensive linebacker, and on special teams. He was an All-American three times, came in third place in voting among Heisman candidates, and won the Maxwell Award, leading to his first-round selection for the Philadelphia Eagles—who, Safarowic notes, shouldn't have been able to grab him. "They were national champs. By all rights it should have been Green Bay or the Giants, but they used to put all the teams' names in a hat. The Eagles drew #1, and they picked Chuck."

Bednarik was a hard guy. While you could assume this level of durability would be where he earned the nickname Concrete Charlie, it was actually a result of his first side job: selling actual concrete, a hustle he continued while playing football, after practice, and during the off-season. "Construction was in its glory in those days," Bednarik said. "I happened to be fortunate to find a job selling ready-mixed concrete, and I did such a good job they said, 'He's as tough as concrete, and he sells it.' So they called me Concrete Charles. It was a job! That's the only reason I did it. It was a good-paying job at that time, it wasn't hard, and it wasn't long." It was an example of the ethics of hard work that had been put into Bednarik from his beginnings. While he was great at football and played like it was all that mattered, he admitted that it was more of a means to an end. "He said it wasn't a big deal for him to play in the NFL," Safarowic says. "He was going to be a teacher. He sold concrete and wine after practice and during the offseason as a professional player. This was a Greatest Generation guy, who was molded by the Depression and World War II. By the time you're twenty-two, you can handle anything."

He would help lead the team to two NFL championships, once in 1949 and again in 1960, a season that would be his most explosive and one he almost didn't play. He considered retiring in February of 1960, but when he realized he was having a fifth daughter, he worried about not having enough money. He stayed in, delivered the Frank Gifford hit, and ended the season with a play that won the Super Bowl—tackling and pinning Green Bay fullback Jim Taylor just eight yards from the goal line, letting the clock run out while Taylor tried to wrestle his way out from under. The game ended 17–13, the Eagles won, and when he let Taylor up from the ground, Bednarik said to him, **"This f***ing game is over."**

Now that Bednarik has passed on, he leaves behind a legacy that sometimes stands at odds with the brash, trash-talking reputation he developed during and after his time in the League. While admitting that in later years Bednarik was known to be "a little crusty," Safarowic remembers a father-in-law who was the most revered person in the room, despite being somewhat insecure and sensitive, in opposition to what many believed from seeing him on TV. "There wasn't anybody that spoke about modern players with more disdain than Chuck. A lot of it was reaction; people wanted to hear him say today's guys are overpaid and underplayed. It wasn't personal resentment or jealousy, just a hardcore, steel mill–gilded edge he had, because nobody could have come from a tougher environment than he did. He was one of the first guys who realized the NFL was in the entertainment industry. He understood showmanship, knew how to spin a story to get a reporter to raise his eyebrows, and he didn't give canned responses."

Safarowic also recalls Bednarik's mouth getting him in trouble, causing long estrangements from the Eagles' owner Norman Braman due to comments he made about the team. Twice he was brought back into the Eagles family by coaches—first by Dick Vermeil, who made him an honorary coach, then again by Andy Reid, after Bednarik's habit of critiquing his old team once again distanced him from the organization. "Look, the guy's from the Archie Bunker generation," Safarowic remembers Reid once saying. "Everybody has relatives like that. I understand him, and I get a kick out of him."

Other controversies were caused by his famous temper, which included cold-cocking fellow teammates who goofed around during calisthenics, duking it out with Chuck Noll from the Cleveland Browns on live national television after a game, and getting into various fistfights on the side of the road. "He had road rage," Safarowic recalls with laughter. "He would come into meetings disheveled. People would ask, 'What happened?' Chuck would say, 'Somebody gave me the finger on the expressway.'"

"It was wonderful for his fans though," Safarowic says. "He would go out of his way and shake their hands, and say, 'Can I sign that for you?' He never high-handed anybody. You could go anywhere with him in Philly—I don't know of any athlete as identifiable with a city as Chuck in Philly. Everybody told stories, including my father and grandfather, all tagging along in his reflected glory. A completely unvarnished character, void of pretense, painfully honest and blunt, who did not have the ability to sidestep or tiptoe around anything in front of him. You always knew exactly where he stood." With a larger-than-life footprint on the game of football, a personality that sometimes seemed abrasive but was always entertaining, and an intense willingness to push himself to do his best at anything he did, Chuck Bednarik gave fans everything he had, mostly because he felt he'd been given so much. One simple quote perhaps best explains who he thanks for a life so full and a legacy as solid as concrete.

"How in the hell did I do it?" he said with a laugh. "That's the way I answer that one—God. Thank you, God."

BOBBY BELL
NO.78

BORN: SHELBY, NORTH CAROLINA
COLLEGE: UNIVERSITY OF MINNESOTA

NFL CAREER: 12 SEASONS
NFL TEAM: KANSAS CITY CHIEFS (1963-1974)
HALL OF FAME INDUCTION: 1983

CAREER HIGHLIGHTS AND AWARDS
NCAA CHAMPIONSHIP (1960)
2× FIRST-TEAM ALL-AMERICAN (1961, 1962)
6× AFL ALL-STAR (1964–1969)
5× FIRST-TEAM ALL-AFL (1965–1969)
SECOND-TEAM ALL-AFL (1964)
2× AFL CHAMPION (1966, 1969)
SUPER BOWL CHAMPION (IV)
AFL ALL-TIME TEAM
3× PRO BOWL (1970–1972)
FIRST-TEAM ALL-PRO (1970)
SECOND-TEAM ALL-PRO (1971)
DEFENSIVE PLAYER OF THE YEAR (1969)
NFL 1970S ALL-DECADE TEAM
1962 OUTLAND TROPHY
UPI COLLEGE FOOTBALL LINEMAN (1962)
NORTH CAROLINA SPORTS HALL OF FAME
MINNESOTA GOLDEN GOPHERS #78 RETIRED

*"I didn't think
I could play
in the NFL.
I went to school
to get my degree,
to go back down
so I could do the
same thing
Mr. Palmer did."*

"I just wanted to be treated like everybody else."

The on field achievements of Bobby Bell, a member of both the College and the Pro Football Hall of Fame, career-long player for the Kansas City Chiefs and Super Bowl winner, have been hard-earned. Time after time, the supremely gifted athlete found ways to prove his worthiness. And though the record shows that Bell's name deserves to be written and spoken along with the greatest football players who've ever lived (which it is), the Shelby, North Carolina native originally had a much simpler idea for what his life would be. He says his goal when he started was just to graduate from school, then get a house, get married, and get a full-time job. "If you did that, you had it made," he says. And though it genuinely seems like Bell would have been fine with a life some consider average, what happened instead was a life full of great achievement.

From growing up in a neighborhood economically dependent on the local textile mill, to becoming one of the football's all-time greats, an ambassador for his hometown, a successful businessman, and a college graduate — in his seventh decade of life — Bell admits he's done more than he ever imagined. If that sounds unbelievably humble or maybe a sign of lacking confidence, it may be easier to understand when you know more about the racial segregation he witnessed from childhood to adulthood. "When I grew up, if I applied for the job, you had to know somebody, or be of a certain color. I guess I learned that the job that I apply for, I have to be ten times better than the next person, if he's white."

Bell never wanted to separate himself from the world. The world was presented to him as a place where divisions were real, regardless of his feelings. It was the control of those feelings that fed his drive to succeed, not only for himself but also for his father, Pink Lee Bell, who was and is a great influence.

"As I was growing up, around twelve or thirteen, I would see people playing golf, and I would ask my dad again, 'Can I play golf like that?' And my dad always said yes. At the time, though, blacks couldn't play golf. We didn't have our own parks, we didn't have swimming pools. But Dad always said, 'Yeah, you can do that! Yeah, you can do that.' That's where it started."

Bell got involved in the local boys' club right around the time a man named Clarence Palmer came to Shelby and built parks specifically for blacks, with baseball fields, swimming pools, boxing rings, and more. When the first swimming pool for blacks opened, Bell became a junior lifeguard. "I was a young kid; I just wanted to experience and see what the outside world was like. And I had no idea I could be a football player, or get a scholarship at a university. I was doing all these odd jobs, working weekends at a local barbecue restaurant called Red Bridge's BBQ, taking and delivering orders to cars. But I had my mind focused on the outside show. What's out there for Bobby Bell?"

While attending the all-black Cleveland High School, Bell worked at the country club owned by the people who owned the town's textile mill, cleaning the grounds and cutting grass. The owners' children liked him and would invite him into their homes to show off their yearbooks. Looking through the pages, he came to realize he was being exposed to something different than his friends knew—the knowledge that some people were somehow able to do different things than everyone else.

"I would go in and see all the sports they were involved with, and I thought, 'Man, this is great!' They were out of town, out of Shelby, out of the state, going to school. My dad never finished school. I would go back home and talk to him, saying, 'Dad, this sounds great! Do you think I would be able to do that?' And my dad would say, 'Yeah, you can do that! It's possible.'

"He always said, 'If you're going to do something, make sure you do it all the way—a hundred and ten percent.' I don't know how he came up with that instead of a hundred percent, but that's what he'd say, a hundred and ten percent or a hundred and twenty percent."

What Bell didn't yet understand was the underlying message his father was delivering. Though he was clearly embedding a work-hard philosophy in young Bobby's mind, he was also explaining to his son a world that was not always fair, particularly when it came to racial realities in the South. The message was that if something was worth doing, it was worth doing the right way, every time, the first time. Bell remembers he would say, "Whatever you do, give it all your best. You've got three strikes against you when you go up to bat. You've gotta make sure if you get a pitch, you knock it out of the ballpark every time."

It wasn't long before Bell began to notice differences on his own. "It took a while for that to sink in, and at first I didn't realize it. Living on my street, all the kids would play together, black and white. But that's because we were young. We were treated different than the whites. In Shelby, you couldn't eat in the restaurants or go to the movies. Or, if you did, you had to go upstairs through the back door, behind the projector. One time when I was 13 years old, we all decided to see a movie together at the same time—the white kids and the black kids. I ran home to tell my mother, and she said, 'You can't go with them.' Because at that time, it was like, this is your place; this is what you do. You didn't cross the lines. That was the first time I was like, 'Oh.' That's when I started reading books and realized it's different out there than what's in Shelby. I didn't understand when I was young why I was getting mistreated. I was a young man just like they were. Why is it different?"

Again, Bell's father provided guidance, explaining the need to take advantage of good situations rather than dwell on the negatives, insisting that if Bobby wanted to compete with people around the world, and not just in Shelby, he had to be on a level playing field and still be better. Ten times better. "And what that meant was that I had to go out and project it. I had to go to the same schools with everybody else. That's what he instilled in me. I had to give it everything. If somebody gave me an opportunity to do something, and I didn't take it, someone else would."

These conversations led to Bell making a commitment to his father that he would leave Shelby to attend a good college or university. His mind was set on being a basketball player since he had the gifts of height and speed. However, he began to show aptitude for other sports, including football and baseball, in his senior year of high school. He even came close to being drafted by the Chicago White Sox, when scouts came to the area and someone suggested they have a look at his team. "When the people came down to look at me to play baseball and assign me to a farm, I told my dad I was going to go play baseball. He said, 'Wait a minute; I thought you wanted to go to a big school and stuff and play basketball in college. I thought you wanted that experience.' I said, 'Well, I can help the family if I go make some money playing baseball.' He said, 'We don't need any help; we're all right.' I told him, 'Well, I can always go back.' And he said to me, 'I don't think you would do it.' He left it to me, and I made the decision that I wanted the college experience.'"

Though naysayers tried to convince him to change his mind, advising him he'd become "just another number and would never make it," he accepted a football scholarship to the University of Minnesota, where he learned to adapt to his environment and outwork his competitors. "I had to make adjustments. Only ten percent of the population in the state of Minnesota was black. Ten percent. There weren't that many black students at the university. I had to overcome the relations thing. I had to learn how to talk to white people. And I promised my dad that if I got a scholarship, I would go on and get my degree. I didn't want to go home."

Bell excelled completely during his college years. He helped the University of Minnesota Gophers win a national championship in 1960 and was named an All-American in both 1961 and 1962, the same year he received the Outland Trophy for his performance as a lineman. He was even a walk-on for the Gophers' basketball team, becoming the first African American basketball player in the school's history.

Still, Bell was not chasing a career in football. Bell had always remained inspired by the impact that Shelby's parks had on his life, and he simply wanted to give back in the same way. "That's what I went to school to be. I didn't go to school to be a football player in the NFL. I didn't think I could play in the NFL. I went to school to get my degree, to go back down so I could do the same thing Mr. Palmer did."

Bell was drafted by the Chiefs before graduating, which may have put off his goal of fulfilling the promise to his father, but it did not deter him from working harder than ever towards new goals. Even as a known player, he worked full-time for General Motors' labor relations department. "I took my vacation during training camp! People said, 'What the heck you doin'? I thought you played football!' I said, 'That's my second job.'" Considering all of his gridiron accolades, and you'd have to assume that, had he continued his career at GM, Bell would surely be the CEO by now.

It's the American Dream, albeit one that is more honest than the television cameras sometimes showed. Bell's all-American story has included good and bad narratives—tales of a country on the cusp of the Civil Rights struggle that defined the times of Bell's athletic heyday. He was involved in a boycott of the 1965 All-Star Game, due to a less-than-hospitable welcome by the host city New Orleans, whose officials made promises that were unkept upon the arrival of the teams' black players. "The NFL told city government, 'Hey, you've gotta do some different things. [Black players have] got to be able to stay in the same hotels, eat in the same restaurants, and all of that. You've gotta do this.' New Orleans said, 'Okay, we'll make the arrangements,' and they agreed to it, but when we flew in there, it wasn't like that.

They did let us check in the hotel room on Bourbon Street, but I went down to the restaurant, and I waited and waited. Finally a black lady came out of the kitchen and said, 'Hey, I'll serve you, you can order stuff, but you've gotta take it to your room.' I said, 'I can't eat it in here?' She said, 'No, you can't eat it here.' I go upstairs and tell the guys, 'Hey man, I don't advocate the stuff going on downstairs. I don't wanna play here if that's the way it is.' All the black players got together and talked, and we chose not to play. And the commissioner went on and moved it to Houston."

Though his position on the field called for constant physical confrontation, Bell played the role of peacekeeper many times, personally going into the streets to calm crowds and quell violence after Dr. Martin Luther King, Jr., was assassinated in 1968. He also doesn't forget moving to Kansas City and being told not only that some restaurants wouldn't serve him, but also that he couldn't live in certain parts of town. "I think I was one of the first blacks to move into Overland Park in 1967 to '68. They didn't want to sell you a house. And the problems don't just go away—they're still there. Back then, you had people who were narrow-minded. To them, everything was A-OK. You could walk into a restaurant, eat, go where you wanted to. You didn't have to go into a colored bathroom instead of a white bathroom. But see, for me, things weren't that way. Down South, you had colored bathrooms. Colored water fountains. We couldn't even drink out of the same water fountains when I was growing up, and I was born here. I was like, wait a minute, is this the world? And you talk about immigrants coming into the country, coming across the border. I was born here. I'm a citizen."

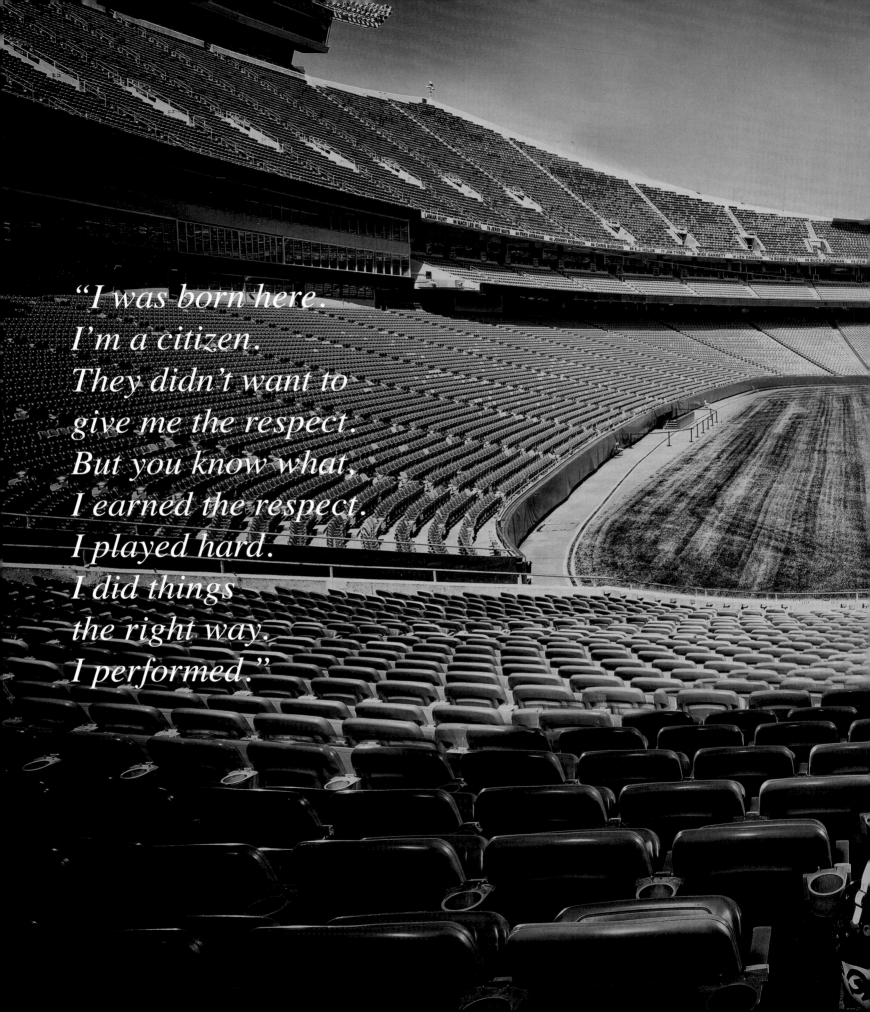

"I was born here.
I'm a citizen.
They didn't want to
give me the respect.
But you know what,
I earned the respect.
I played hard.
I did things
the right way.
I performed."

Though he's still unsettled by what he sees as lingering issues of inequality, Bell has also reminded himself to savor the good times. While he could call out his college championship, Super Bowl victory or All-Star selections as the greatest moments of his career, there are two others that stand apart, and both include his father. The first, which he has called "the top of the pyramid," was when he went back and finished his college degree at 74 years old. "I looked at the wall in my man cave one day. I had all these awards and stuff. But I thought to myself, 'Wait a minute. I promised my dad I'd get a degree.' So that's what I did. And it's the best thing I ever did."

The other highlight was having his father see him play live in what would end up being University of Minnesota's national championship game against Wisconsin. It was the first time Pink Lee Bell had the opportunity to see his son Bobby play a big school, and it was in front of more than 60,000 others. "We'd talked about me going to a big school, and here was his son, playing in a big game. He thought the world of that." Unfortunately, luck would have it that Bobby would crack three ribs before halftime, an injury that should have taken him out of the game. "I went into the locker room, and they had me laying on the table. Dad walked in wearing his top coat. He talked to the trainer first, and the trainer said, 'Yeah, he can play. It'll just be some pain. We're going to tape him up anyway.' He looked at me and said, 'Look boy, I didn't come all this way to see you laying up on this table.' And I said, 'Yes, sir,' and I went out after halftime. I sat on the bench for the first play. I looked over my shoulder at the seats behind me, and I saw my dad sitting there. And I said, 'Ohhhhhh, crap.'"

Without even thinking, without even saying anything—nobody knew, the coaches or the players—Bell ran out on the field during a time-out. He told one of the tackles, "Hey, you're out, I'm in." The player replied, "Hey man, aren't you hurt?" Bell's answer: "Man, you're out. You're out."

"And I played the rest of the game. With some cracked ribs, man. I had to play. He's there, and I'm not playing? Come on… That was the highlight of my career. I know I've played in a couple of Super Bowls and stuff, but that was the highlight. It made him so proud. He would walk out on the streets of Shelby and people white and black would holler to him. 'Hey, Pink! I saw your son on TV last night in the game. He was great, man!' Then it was like, 'He's one of us now.' It's like the whole town took me under its wings. That was the change. And it was because, I wanna think, I did the right thing."

Bell's name is now one of five on the stadium at University of Minnesota, where he also has a locker room and a scholarship in his name. When he was given the key to the city of Shelby, he didn't miss the opportunity to remind those gathered in the town square that before he became an adult, all he ever wanted was the opportunity to cross Main Street to get a cup of ice cream like other children his age.

When he's not opening a new barbecue restaurant, raising money for NFL-affiliated charities or practicing golf, he gives motivational speeches to youth, offering heavy helpings of hope with lots of hard work. He tells young people to reinvent themselves and make constant adjustments to become better. And he advises them to remain positive throughout all the challenges. "That's what I had to do in life," he says. "You've gotta work harder, you've gotta do certain things. I wanted to do the right thing. I didn't want to get all pissed off at the world and stuff, you know? This was the way it had to go. If you do the right thing, they've gotta come along with you, otherwise they look stupid, you know? They didn't want to give me the respect. But you know what, I earned the respect. I played hard. I did things the right way. I performed. They could count on me any week. And with that attitude I played every game. Respect me as a human being."

CORNELIUS BENNETT
NO.**97**

BORN: BIRMINGHAM, ALABAMA

COLLEGE: UNIVERSITY OF ALABAMA

NFL CAREER: 14 SEASONS

NFL TEAM: INDIANAPOLIS COLTS (1987)

TRADED TO BUFFALO BILLS (1987-1995),

ATLANTA FALCONS (1996-1998), INDIANAPOLIS COLTS (1999-2000)

CAREER HIGHLIGHTS AND AWARDS

5× PRO BOWL (1988, 1990–1993)

3× ALL-PRO (1988, 1991, 1992)

4× AFC CHAMPION (1990–1993)

NFC CHAMPION (1998)

2× AFC DEFENSIVE PLAYER OF THE YEAR (1988, 1991)

NFL 1990S ALL-DECADE TEAM

BUFFALO BILLS 50TH ANNIVERSARY TEAM

3× FIRST-TEAM ALL-AMERICAN (1984–1986)

3× ALL-SEC (1984–1986)

SEC PLAYER OF THE YEAR (1986)

LOMBARDI AWARD (1986)

ALABAMA SPORTS HALL OF FAME

"As everything progressed, every day there was some kind of comparison to L.T., and I really didn't know who L.T. was, honestly. So I had to investigate. I found out who he was and I was like, Holy... you know what. That was some great praise."

"I didn't play to be in the Hall of Fame. I played because I loved playing football."

You hear nothing but truth when Cornelius Bennett speaks about the proverbial elephant in the locker room from his former career as a linebacker for the Buffalo Bills, Atlanta Falcons and Indianapolis Colts. Even though as a five-time Pro Bowler, four-time AFC champion, three-time All-Pro player, two-time AFC Defensive Player of the Year, and member of both the Buffalo Bills 50th Anniversary Team and the NFL's 1990s All-Decade Team, you might expect to hear frustration in his voice about one particular missing part of his career story. Instead, Bennett has a simple way to explain his motivation to excel in football, and it doesn't hinge on being included in the Pro Football Hall of Fame.

"I played because I realized in 1979 that I had a gift, and I wanted to give it to the world. All the other stuff is just stuff. If it happens, man, so be it. Everything else that came with it just happened to be there. I ain't miss nothing."

Cornelius Bennett certainly didn't miss the moment that set him on a path toward greatness -- the day he realized he could play football with and against anybody. It was Thanksgiving Day 1979, back in his hometown of Birmingham, Alabama. "I was 14 and we were playing in a park against these grown men: my family of men against a neighborhood. Now, my family is a family of big men. I had three uncles that we called "Woot," "Wop" and "Wham" from their high school football days, and some cousins. But I had an all-pro day. I think I scored six touchdowns and God knows how many tackles. I realized I wasn't scared to be out there against grown men from the first throw of the game.

And we didn't kickoff; we threw off, with them returning it. And this wasn't touch-football -- this was gridiron, sandlot football. Running down the field, making the first tackle, there was no fear in my mind and no fear in my heart. I wasn't afraid to do anything out there that day.

I remember riding back, on the back of a pickup truck, to my grandmother's house for Thanksgiving dinner. Everybody was congratulating me on how I played, and I felt really good about how I played against these grown men. That's the first time I ever realized I had something special. I thought, 'Wow, I can really play football.' I'd always kinda doubted myself, but after that day it was dedication."

Bennett excelled at different positions going into high school. He could throw a football with the best of them, and learned to be quick on his toes from tackling, and running away from, his cousins and brothers. Still, he says he was only marginally good until midway through his junior year when his high school coach played him at running back, since the team wasn't winning much anyway. "That's really when I started being noticed by major schools and I realized I could go on to play college football." He recalls the phone calls and snail mail he received while being recruited, and remembers one of the particularly funny challenges he faced. "At the time I'd never been on an airplane, or really outside the state of Alabama, and I was afraid to fly. I didn't think that wherever I went I was gonna have to get on an airplane," he says, laughing harder. "At the time, trying to make sense to my 17-year-old self, wherever I go they're going to have to put me on a bus and let me arrive two days early. That's how ignorant I was at the time."

Recruited by Paul "Bear" Bryant, he chose to play for the University of Alabama. "The expectation for myself was just to make the travel team and play some." But since Bennett was big and fast, the expectations from the coaches were totally different, which he discovered after his first practice with the Crimson Tide. They saw similarities to another superstar linebacker – Lawrence Taylor – and wanted to find out if he could live up to the challenge. "As everything progressed, every day there was some kind of comparison to L.T., and I really didn't know who L.T. was, honestly. So I had to investigate. I found out who he was and I was like, "Holy... you know what." That was some great praise.

Bennett certainly did not disappoint. He was a three-time All-SEC player, a three-time first-team All-American (only one other Alabama player, Woodrow Lowe, ever did the same), and spent his senior year in 1986 winning SEC Player of the Year honors, as well as the Lombardi Award, which is given to the year's best college lineman or linebacker. But it only makes sense that the standout moment of his college career, when he really knew he was different, was during his freshman year while playing against Bo Jackson and Alabama's famous archrival: the Auburn Tigers. "For some reason the coaches at Alabama decided they wanted the seniors to get some playing time. In two of the few plays I missed in the game Bo scored long touchdowns. I always wondered if he would have scored had I been in the game. I always felt that when I played against an athlete like Bo I was the only person who had a chance to stop them. I always felt like if I started chasing someone, they weren't gonna get away. You'd never see on a film that if I was chasing behind someone I didn't catch them. So that's how I felt with Bo, but that's how I've always felt my whole career. You put me against their best, I'm gonna win."

When it came time to go pro, Bennett wasn't only concerned about winning the game on the field, holding perhaps an even tougher line during contract negotiations than he did at the line of scrimmage. "As a kid you're not thinking about the money or the negotiation. All you're thinking about is being on TV on Sunday. But I felt I had something impeding me from fulfilling my dream, so throughout the whole course of negotiating and holding out, that was the main thing, like, 'Man, here I am. I can't let anything happen to me to keep me from living this dream.' So I tried to protect myself from any hurt, harm or danger throughout that whole process of holding out. Here I am, this kid from Birmingham who grew up with nothing, getting a chance to live out a dream.

Every kid I knew wanted to be a professional football player. Not some of them -- every kid I knew. And I've got money in the wake of it." He took it seriously.

The result was that Bennett was traded to the Buffalo Bills, and began the career that may not have included a Super Bowl ring, but proved that he was an impact player who brought out the best in every team for whom he played. He accomplished this using all of his natural talent and ability, as well as making use of the locker room – an environment where he could exert influence, and develop bonds between himself and his teammates. He remembers Buffalo's 1988 season, when they were known as "The Bickering Bills" due to post-game arguments that spilled out into the public, and how the negative energy was turned around in the locker room a year later, resulting in the beginning of an infamous run that included four consecutive AFC championships starting in 1990. When he left the team to play for Atlanta in 1996, the same strategy was applied, which helped the Falcons go from 3-13 his first year to leading the team to its first Super Bowl appearance ever, just two years later.

"The lesson I took from that first year was that everything I learned in Buffalo, I charged myself to teach it to the Chuck Smiths, and the Bob Whitfields, and Jamal Andersons, of the Falcons, because that hadn't been taught there. There was no locker room presence from anyone in Atlanta. Everybody was doing their own thing. Me being 30 years old when I got there, I felt it was my duty to change the whole outlook. You've gotta have that locker room.

"I try to teach my 16-year-old son, 'You're gonna be a great player and always be around great players, but can y'all play together and be great?' Because if you can't be great together, it doesn't matter. I could always tell the character of a person and figure out what kind of player you were going to be, and whether or not we were going to become locker room mates or whatever, from sitting with you for a long time. To me it means so much; it's part of what's missing in football." Bennett believes the loss of locker room energy after the Falcons' Super Bowl loss was the most damaging element in terms of team momentum. "I know for a fact that, had Eugene Robinson and myself stuck around for another year, Atlanta could have went back for another Super Bowl. I strongly believe it. But they lost the locker room presence. I've heard guys say it, and I've heard that Coach Reeves said it, although he's never said it around me."

Even as he came full-circle to play for Indianapolis at the end of his career, he stuck to that philosophy and helped set the tone for what many people already considered to be Peyton Manning's team. "I kinda came in at a good time, but again, a team that had gone 3-13 the year before I got there. I thank God I wasn't there for that, but I came in with the same attitude I had in Atlanta -- change the atmosphere. At 34 years old, even though I knew the locker room would be Peyton's, he was still a young kid at the time. It was gonna be mine no matter what. From day one I took control. I led us to a 13-3 season that year, and I had one of my finest seasons of football at 34 years old, with a bad knee."

So even as he would clearly appreciate being included, he says he knows why his name and number have not yet been called to join the Pro Football Hall of Fame. "I think it's stat-driven," he says. And I don't want to be judged on stats because I didn't play the game for stats. I think that people doing the voting, that's all they have to go on, because they weren't on the field with us. The tight ends I played, the voters could never feel me snatching them, and jerkin' 'em, and pounding their heads into the turf. They can't feel that. All they've got is papers in front of them, and they see Cornelius Bennett and Derrick Thomas, they see L.T., they see Rickey Jackson, Andre Tippet -- all these new-age outside linebackers. And they start comparing, and all those guys have 100 or more sacks, and I'm way down there at like 70. They're like, what basically has he done? They're not gonna question the guys I played against. They're not going to ask my teammates, because if they did I'd have been in a long time ago."

It was his strength, speed and versatility, not to mention his lack of selfishness, that Bennett says impacted those statistics. He knew he could play more than one position, so he did. "To me, that was one of the reasons I couldn't get 100 sacks. Because I could do so much else, and I enjoyed it. One thing I'm very proud of, in my mind and my heart, is that not one coach I ever had can say that if they came up to me and said, 'This is what I want you to do,' I would say, 'No, I don't want to.' And I could have; I had enough star-status. I could have pulled some selfishness, but I refused to be that person. I didn't grow up playing that way, and didn't like to be around selfish players. If that keeps me from being in the Hall of Fame, so be it." These are the accomplishments that make Cornelius Bennett most proud of his time in the NFL. Though he was constantly compared to L.T., he says, "I knew I could only be Cornelius Bennett. And Cornelius Bennett had one speed, and that was full-speed. I might have been a little unorthodox in certain parts of my game, but I always found the best way to get the job done. I figured that out early on from that Thanksgiving Day in 1979. Fast-forward to today, and when he looks back, he doesn't see any slights from Hall of Fame voters, or missing Super Bowl rings. He sees the real victory, and knows he's won in ways that can't be quantified by numbers in statistician's logs or even dollars he was paid to be one of pro football's all-time greats.

"All I know is that when I'm around my teammates, the love I get when I see Thurman, Bruce, Jim, Andre and Darryl, and the well-wishes, and the 'hope so's, and 'it's gonna come' – that means more to me than anything in the world. Even the young linebackers I was able to groom, those kids tell me, 'You don't know how much you meant to me. You showed me how to be a professional.'"

"Man, those things right there, that's the Hall of Fame to me."

DERRICK BROOKS
NO.55

BORN: PENSACOLA, FLORIDA
COLLEGE: FLORIDA STATE UNIVERSITY

NFL CAREER: 14 SEASONS
NFL TEAM: TAMPA BAY BUCCANEERS (1995-2008)
HALL OF FAME INDUCTION: 2014

CAREER HIGHLIGHTS AND AWARDS
11× PRO BOWL (1997–2006, 2008)
9× ALL-PRO (1997–2005)
SUPER BOWL CHAMPION (XXXVII)
WALTER PAYTON MAN OF THE YEAR AWARD (2000)
AP NFL DEFENSIVE PLAYER OF THE YEAR (2002)
NFL ALUMNI LINEBACKER OF THE YEAR (2002)
"WHIZZER" WHITE NFL MAN OF THE YEAR AWARD(2003)
PRO BOWL MVP (2005)
NFL 2000S ALL-DECADE TEAM
TAMPA BAY BUCCANEERS RING OF HONOR
TAMPA BAY BUCCANEERS #55 RETIRED
FLORIDA STATE SEMINOLES #10 RETIRED
USA TODAY HIGH SCHOOL ALL-AMERICAN (1990)
BOWL COALITION NATIONAL CHAMPION (1993)
2× CONSENSUS ALL-AMERICAN (1993–2004)

"Put God first in all you do, and treat others the way you want 'em to treat you. Commit everything you do unto the Lord and your plans will succeed."

"All those accomplishments between the white lines on the field...
the underlying desire really had nothing to do with sports."

Derrick Brooks says he's always been a self-motivated person, yet it still may surprise fans to know that he credits academia more than athletics for what he has learned and what he has been able to do before and after his professional playing career.

"One embarrassing term I took in the late eighties/early nineties, and really hated, was 'dumb jock.' I remember the story of Dexter Manley, [the defensive end nicknamed Secretary of Defense, who admitted he couldn't read as a college student], and people's perception of athletes. I was already self-motivated through education, but this really was a burning fire for me, so I used that self-motivation throughout my entire life. In high school, I was the only African-American in a lot of my honors classes, but yet I was taking on the sword, saying, 'I'm gonna make the highest grades and be the smartest kid. And still play football.'"

Derrick had strong family support growing up, which was sometimes expressed as tough love. "When I was being a class clown, despite how much success I was having in sports at the time, or being the smartest kid in the class, my dad let me know if I didn't know how to act or treat people, I was gonna end up in one of two places: in jail or in the graveyard, and he showed me by putting the belt on me.

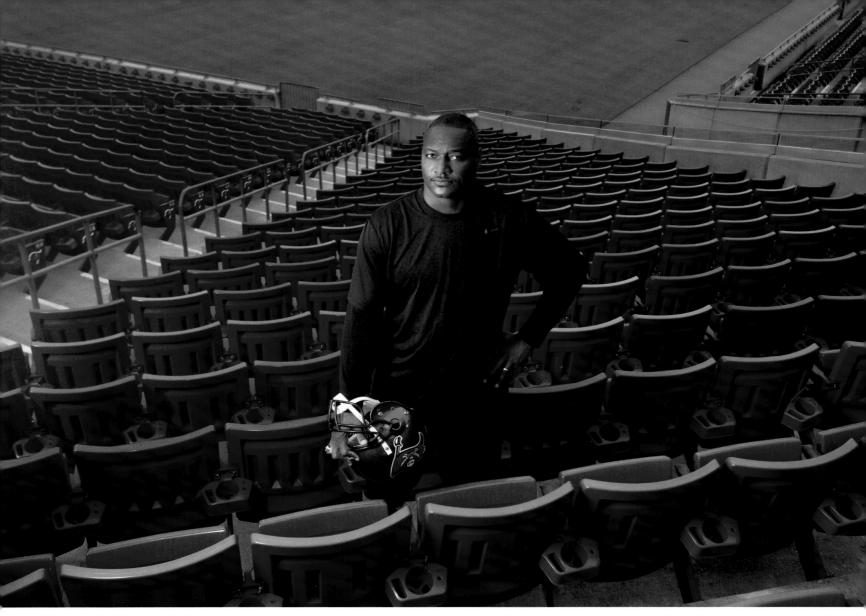

"I thank God that my dad loved me enough to whoop me in the fifth grade in front of my class, but that was the last time he whooped me." It was that fork in the road, where he stood up and said, 'You're gonna stand for something, because you're gonna stop this foolishness.' Today if we do that, we'll get killed. We'll go to jail." He laughs.

His grandmother was also a big inspiration for the person he has become. "My grandmother was a serious lady. She just had a way about how she went about her life. Her life saying is how I live my life today: 'Put God first in all you do, and treat others the way you want 'em to treat you.' You're talking about a lady who people depended on, for a lot of things—she was there. She set that standard of giving. And when I carry her spirit in me, that's what it's all about, representing that last name. She said, 'Always understand that it means something, and never take it for granted.'"

Having the same hometown as Emmitt Smith, one of the NFL's all-time greatest running backs (and whose high school offensive coordinator Jimmy Nichols was Derrick's high school head coach), also spurred Derrick's ambition to excel. "Emmitt always set a standard that I wanted to chase, and revel in the journey of chasing. In between our football success, I think we've done it in a special way because we've always recognized our hometown, and anything we've been able to accomplish, we always take time to recognize Pensacola, Florida."

Derrick acknowledges the presence of a higher power in this connection, saying he believes God "aligned a lot of stars for us to have very similar career paths." Deeply rooted in his Christian faith, Derrick even shares a favorite Bible verse—Proverbs 16:3—in the signature of every email or text message he sends. "'Commit everything you do unto the Lord and your plans will succeed.' Anything you do, you have to involve God to give yourself a fifty percent chance of achieving it or not failing. I believe that verse transcends anything and anybody, and it breaks down barriers."

Brooks' well-documented, barrier-like defensive skills made him a legendary linebacker. At Florida State University, he helped the 1993 team win a national championship against Nebraska and was named a first-team All-American during his final two years; however, he never allowed football to distract him from taking advantage of the educational opportunity at the university. "The football success, I knew that was something I couldn't control. At Florida State, the greatest of the greatest were being recruited year-in and year-out. What could I do to set myself apart and make sure I had the value of my time in Tallahassee? It was about my grades. I could control my grades. No coach, no teacher, no one else but me. And I wanted to maximize that. Once I understood how prestigious that was, man…to set yourself apart in that arena, and now that's what you're gonna be doing in life no matter what happens in football—it took on a bigger role for me. So when I saw those Academic All-Americans, I looked at my teammates and I kinda put myself off to the side like, 'Thank you guys, but this is a walk I have to take by myself.' A lot more sacrifices were made in terms of my academic balance than my athletic balance. That environment is controlled; you already know the sacrifices and you've got brothers with you to go through it.

"But you're talking about studying for a test, you've got a twenty-page final that's due, you're not leaning on nobody. My professors didn't want to hear I was stuck at practice from two to six. They wanted to see the results. Some guys really struggled with that. I guess in my mental makeup, it was an easy decision to make. What's more important? Faith, family, football—in that order. And education is a part of all of them. And hey, it's gonna always be about your education first. If you happen to be good in sports or taking to football, so be it."

He went on to achieve his goal of becoming an Academic All-American at FSU, earning a bachelor's degree in three years and a master's in business communication in 1999, while playing in college and the NFL. He spent his entire career with the Tampa Bay Buccaneers, making 11 Pro Bowl appearances, helping the team win its first Super Bowl championship in 2003, and receiving honors including AP Defensive Player of the Year in 2002 and Pro Bowl MVP in 2005. Throughout his pro career, Brooks was recognized and honored for his humanitarian efforts, character, and leadership, with the NFL's Walter Payton Man of the Year Award in 2000, the Bart Starr Award in 2003, and the Byron "Whizzer" White award in 2004.

Today, as founder of the Brooks-DeBartolo Collegiate High School, and the Brooks Bunch charity and youth scholarship foundation, Brooks takes a "mobile classroom" approach, flying young adults across America and internationally, presenting them with a firsthand experience of life beyond their immediate surroundings and the wealth of information available around the world. He also works with the March of Dimes, the drug-deterrent D.A.R.E. program, and other organizations that help students prepare for life after high school.

Out of everything he learned along the way, Brooks believes humility is one of the most important lessons to pass on to others. He recalls being named MVP of his high school football team and proudly telling everyone. "My dad, with his sixth grade education, got home one day and said, 'Son, let me tell you one thing. When you toot your own horn, you make one sound. And it don't last, because you run out of breath. But when everybody else is tooting your horn, that sound never ends.' I think of things from that perspective, and really treating others how I want to be treated. I believe in that humble approach. When you're humble, you get a lot more things accomplished, because others understand you're putting them in the same light, or a better light, than yourself."

When it's all said and done, the god-fearing husband and father of four hopes to be remembered for giving his all in everything—not just defending his team's end zone, but teaching others to find the inner strength to tackle their own goals.

"Those are the memories," Brooks says of his football career. "I would like to think all these accomplishments don't mean anything if what I've done didn't invest into kids being better citizens. I want to motivate people to achieve more with what they have, because everybody has time. You don't need a boatload of money to make a difference. You need a willing heart, and you need time. If you have those two, I believe you can change the world."

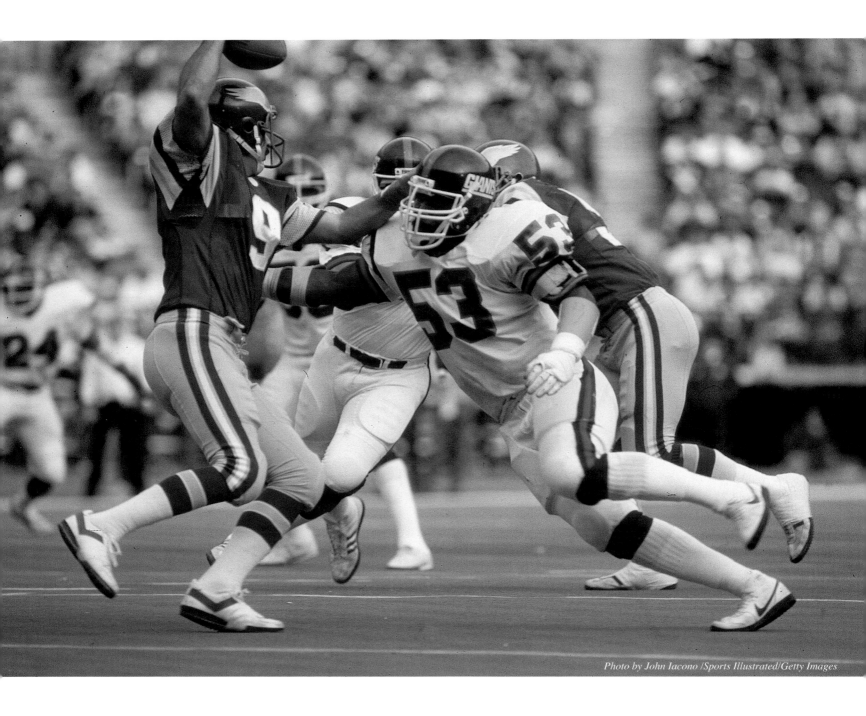

HARRY CARSON
NO.53

BORN: FLORENCE, SOUTH CAROLINA
COLLEGE: SOUTH CAROLINA STATE

NFL CAREER: 12 SEASONS
NFL TEAM: NEW YORK GIANTS (1976-1988)
HALL OF FAME INDUCTION: 2006

CAREER HIGHLIGHTS AND AWARDS
9× PRO BOWL (1978, 1979, 1981–1987)
2× FIRST-TEAM ALL-PRO (1981, 1984)
4× SECOND-TEAM ALL-PRO (1978, 1982, 1985, 1986)
SUPER BOWL CHAMPION (XXI)
NEW YORK GIANTS RING OF HONOR
PRO FOOTBALL HALL OF FAME
COLLEGE FOOTBALL HALL OF FAME

"I'm just another guy that had the opportunity to do something rather extraordinary."

"Football is what I did, not what I am."

When Harry Carson set out to write a book, he chose to name it *Captain for Life*, encompassing more than just his experiences on the football field. Yes, he was voted into the Pro Football Hall of Fame in 2006, just as he had been voted into the College Football Hall of Fame in 2002. The Super Bowl ring from 1987—a game in which he and the New York Giants soundly defeated John Elway's Broncos by 19 points—fits only his finger. Just like the Ring of Honor he was given by the Giants, with whom he spent his entire professional career. Carson made the decision to title his autobiography based on one simple thing: honesty.

"I was never a violent person. I probably never should have played football, because I was never really built to be a football player. My mind-state was never built to be hitting people or to hurt people. Football was something I fell into. I went to school to get an education, not to play football. If it was solely about football, then I would be at a loss now, because at some point you've gotta give it up. You can't play football forever."

While Carson jokes about having other motivations as well ("It was about girls," he says with a smile), he says he always wanted to talk more about life after the game. He's firm when he says the real story is in how he lived his life before and after the game, between the future he created and the foundation he received as a kid growing up in Florence, South Carolina. "It was just guys hanging out. We couldn't afford a football, so you just put some rocks in a small milk carton—that was the football. You didn't have teams. Whoever picked up the football, they got smashed by everybody else. You learned how to elude people and utilize your agility and speed. If you didn't have the quickness you'd be one of those power rushers. Guys would jump on your back. They couldn't bring you down, and you would drag them. It was just about having fun. It wasn't so much about being in love with playing football. It was just me hanging out with my friends and trying to make do with what we had."

His athletic gifts provided opportunities to grow and experience things beyond his own cultural surroundings and humble upbringing. He went to predominately African American schools until his sophomore year, when he was zoned to attend McClenaghan High, where he acclimated himself to a different environment and quickly showed aptitude as a leader. "I became one of the chairmen of the biracial committee, because with football you bring people together to accomplish a goal. It doesn't matter whether you're a linebacker, offensive or defensive lineman, or a secondary running back; everybody comes together from different places, all over. You wear that uniform and it doesn't matter who you are. You're trying to bring everyone together and be civil with one another. You're in it for the same goal: you want everybody to get along, do their best, live amongst each other civilly, and ultimately graduate and go on to live a productive life."

He recalls initially running into difficulty because some peers "didn't really embrace change," but he says eventually everyone got on board. "We put color aside and just worked together." The simple yet eloquent way Carson expresses thoughts and memories might seem extraordinary to anyone who hasn't had the opportunity to get to know him. But his childhood experience should sound immediately familiar to anyone who's heard the African proverb, 'It takes a village to raise a child.' Back in the fifties, when I grew up, I had my mom and dad, but there were people in the community who, if I did something wrong, would get after me. I could get a whipping from them, then go home and get another whipping, because they would tell my parents what I did."

He says this motivated him to be a good kid "for the most part," along with the feeling that he owed it to those people to live up to his potential. One of his fondest memories from growing up in Florence was when the only black doctor in his hometown gave him advice, after refusing payment for giving Carson a physical examination—something he needed in order to officially join the Bulldogs of South Carolina State University as a linebacker.

"My sister gave me some money to pay the doctor. At the end [of the exam], I went to give him the money, and he said, 'Boy, I don't want your money. I want you to make something of your life.'

"That's something I've always remembered, Carson says. "I've always felt the sense of community and belonging to more than just me. These people had a vested interest in me. I often think about where I came from and how these people really wanted the best for me." Carson paid them all back by finishing college and never missing a game during his four years as a South Carolina State Bulldog. He also led the team defense to deliver six shutout games in his senior year, as well as an NCAA record on points allowed by opponents for the 10-game season.

Carson, who earned a Bachelor of Science degree in education from South Carolina State, says he "went in as a kid and came out a man," learning much about himself and the game of football. That knowledge, he says, includes how the sport was simply a vehicle to drive his ambitions and how it would eventually lead to the end of a road. He sees this today in the form of the NFL Draft.

"All these guys are gonna come out there and wear the hat, hug the commissioner, give him some dap and everything. But nobody sees four or five years down the road, where they're walking out of the complex and all their stuff is in a garbage bag."

He also compares playing in the NFL to leasing a car. "If you don't take care of it, you'll have all these problems with the engine, the computer system, and all this stuff going on with the interior. People look at me and say, 'Man, you still look great!' And I appreciate the compliment, but they don't know what's going on in the inside. Everybody who plays leaves with something. For the most part you're leasing out your body, and you don't necessarily know what you're giving up as a result, or how it's going to affect you down the road."

"I've got a big mouth. Sometimes it bruises people because I don't always have a filter, but I let the chips fall where they may."

Carson's mind remains capable of such brilliant analogies even though he was diagnosed with post-concussion syndrome, or PCS, in 1990. "For many guys, it's their knees, their ankles and hips. All that stuff can be replaced. But for so many others it's the brain, and you can't replace the brain. I've lived it. I learned how to live with this condition, with a relatively normal life. When I share with my former teammates, I come from experience. They trust me enough to listen to what I have to say. And hopefully they won't do what Junior Seau did. Or Ray Easterling did."

Just as the title of his book suggests, Carson sees himself as a resource to help others. He feels a certain responsibility to acknowledge Easterling, who like Seau committed suicide and was found to have suffered from chronic traumatic encephalopathy, or CTE. "He reached out to me, and I couldn't help him. I passed him on to someone else to help. Within a year he shot himself. If I had known he was in that place where he felt he had no place to turn, I would have interceded." He seems to particularly regret missing Easterling's window of vulnerability—something he knows is rare among NFL players. "When players play the game, we are very proud men. I never want a man, especially a man who has played football, to lose his dignity. When a man or a football player acknowledges that he has some mental or neurological issues, trust me, it takes a lot to acknowledge they're at that point, so you'd better do something to help. We don't share our weaknesses. And so, for a man or player to share what they're going through at the time with me, I hold that sacred. That's part of what being a captain is. And quite frankly, one of the greatest things I can be doing right now is advocating for those who don't think they have a voice. Because once you leave the league, you have no voice. You're gone. A lot of teams close that door, and that door is closed forever. When it's over, it's over."

So Carson puts his voice, and the great respect he has earned, to good use, even when that means having the uncomfortable conversations that will lead to positive change. "I have no problem saying things that need to be said, doing things that need to be done, being fair and honest with people. I hope they can take things that I say in a way that I'm not bashing them. I've lived and experienced certain things. I've got a big mouth. Sometimes it bruises people because I don't always have a filter, but I let the chips fall where they may." Maybe it's because of the toughness he developed through the game, but whatever the origin, he has turned this toughness into a philosophy that informs his entire life and outlook.

"Football really is a microcosm of life. There are so many things in football you take with you. One of the key things on the football field is sometimes you are going to get hit, and when you get hit, it's gonna be really, really hard. Like a wide receiver coming across the middle, whether it's a free safety or a linebacker, you get an opportunity to hit that guy when he goes up for the ball. When you hit him, the crowd goes, 'Woooo,' because they can see it. That guy has to get up. He may not want to get up, and he may be hurting, but whether it's for show or whatever, he has to get up. The same is true in life. You're gonna get hit so hard, and you're gonna have to get up. Whether it's something medical, or with your child, it might be a divorce you go through, it's gonna hit you so hard you're gonna want to just lay there and waddle. But you've gotta get up. So football really does toughen you up and prepare you for what you have to go through. There are so many lessons you get from the game that are so valuable. It's not just about the physicality on the field, it's knowing what you have to do within a fraction of a second, and make a decision. I wish you could bottle up those lessons and distribute them to all kids everywhere to make them tough and smart, but unfortunately you have to go through it and learn it. And when you learn it, it sticks with you for the rest of your life."

Now in his early sixties, Carson shares this message wherever he goes, with anyone who needs to hear it. That ranges from reuniting with fellow retired players, whether there's cause for celebration or a need for support, to visiting correctional facilities, where he speaks to incarcerated young men and motivates them to look toward a brighter future. That's what captains do, from start to finish.

"I try to be an inspiration. I give of myself and give as much knowledge as I can. I'm not a flamboyant person. I'm just another guy that had the opportunity to do something rather extraordinary. Somebody had to lead the way."

LONDON FLETCHER
NO.59

BORN: CLEVELAND, OHIO
COLLEGE: JOHN CARROLL UNIVERSITY

NFL CAREER: 12 SEASONS
NFL TEAM: SAINT LOUIS RAMS (1998-2001), BUFFALO BILLS (2002-2006),
WASHINGTON REDSKINS (2007-2013)

CAREER HIGHLIGHTS AND AWARDS
SUPER BOWL CHAMPION (XXXIV)
2× NFC CHAMPION (1999, 2001)
4× PRO BOWL (2009–2012)
2× SECOND-TEAM ALL-PRO (2011, 2012)
NFL COMBINED TACKLES LEADER (2011)
BART STARR MAN OF THE YEAR AWARD (2012)
NFC DEFENSIVE PLAYER OF THE MONTH (DECEMBER 2012)
NFL RECORD FOR CONSECUTIVE STARTS AT LINEBACKER (215)
NFL RECORD FOR CONSECUTIVE GAMES PLAYED AT LINEBACKER (256)
MOST TACKLES FROM 2000–2009 (1,244)
ST. LOUIS RAMS ROOKIE OF THE YEAR (1998)
ST. LOUIS RAMS 10TH ANNIVERSARY TEAM

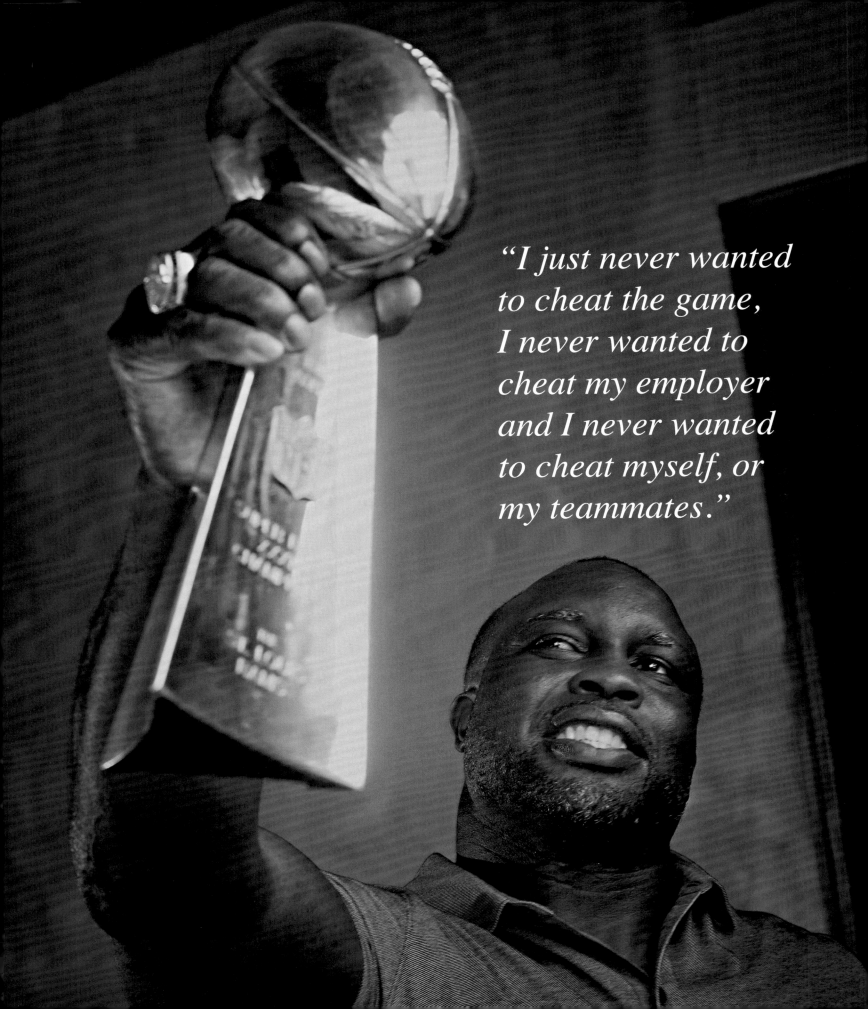

"I just never wanted to cheat the game, I never wanted to cheat my employer and I never wanted to cheat myself, or my teammates."

"I just couldn't let Romanowski have that record."

London Fletcher is reliable. As the current record-holder for most consecutive NFL games played in the linebacker position, he's someone who, after making a promise to anyone—including himself—can be counted on to deliver. You might even say he takes his determination to the level of a vendetta. Whatever the motivation, he makes the commitment, achieves his goals, and sets standards, regardless of whether gratification is delayed or instantly granted.

"After my 15th season, I was about four games short of Bill Romanowski," Fletcher says. "He had the record. I thought long and hard about retiring before my 16th season. I had been away from my family, and I had a couple injuries I was dealing with. If I was gonna play again, I was going to need surgery. And I was having a hard time trying to find motivation, like, 'Do I really wanna go through with this?'

"And then I thought about Romanowski having the record, and he's an admitted steroid user. Then I was like, 'Do I want this guy being the guy who holds the record? Hell no.' I felt like I owed it to the game to go and play at least five more games to break his record, just so he wouldn't be the guy."

Fletcher not only claimed the record, but his grand total of 256 consecutive games makes him one of only four players in the history of the NFL to play so long without missing a kickoff. He's not only shown up; he's shown out and proven his talent since day one of his pro career. He debuted in 1998, signing with the St. Louis Rams. Although he joined the team as an undrafted free agent, he played all 16 games of the season and went on to be named the team's Rookie of the Year. The following season, as starting middle linebacker, he led their defense in tackles and helped the Rams defeat the Tennessee Titans in Super Bowl XXXIV.

The 1999 season would also be Fletcher's first time being picked as an alternate to the Pro Bowl, and the start of a frustrating period of high output that never seemed to be enough to help him meet a very particular goal: the NFL Pro Bowl. Eleven times in his 16 seasons he was named a Pro Bowl alternate, but he didn't get to play in the game until 2010, when Saints player Jonathan Vilma had to skip it due to Super Bowl obligations. Repeatedly not being named a first-team Pro Bowler continued throughout his time in the NFL, despite an illustrious career that saw him set a franchise record for tackles in his first season with the Buffalo Bills, then Defensive Captain and later Defensive Player of the Year for the Washington Redskins after signing with the team in 2008—again, while never missing a game. Being snubbed for so long caused Fletcher to tell reporters in 2008 about a nickname he'd given himself—one that friends, teammates, and fans still remember and laugh about today—"the Susan Lucci of the NFL." Looking back, Fletcher laughs and credits lessons from his childhood with helping to prepare him for tests later in life, many of which pale in comparison to his upbringing.

Growing up in inner-city Cleveland, Ohio, Fletcher was the middle child of five. He was raised in a lower-income neighborhood, in a three-story house with not only his immediate family but also his grandparents, his cousins, and his aunt. He recalls being uncomfortably close to many aspects of the streets—drugs, violence, early childhood pregnancy, and other realities that severely affected those close to him. For most of his childhood and teenage years, his older brother would be in and out of jail. His family would also experience a devastating loss: his older sister, who dropped out of school and struggled with addiction, was only 18 when she was found dead after being raped and murdered. It was a tragedy that profoundly affected his mother, who fell into a deep depression and turned to drugs.

Fletcher, who was 14 years old at the time, took inventory and made a promise to himself, for his mother's benefit more than his own: he would be the first in their family to graduate college. "I put it in my mind that I would bring a smile to her face," he says.

Using sports as a possible ticket to college, he started playing basketball seriously, accepting a scholarship to play for Saint Francis University in Pennsylvania. Later he transferred to Ohio's John Carroll University, a Division III school, even though Division I schools offered him a football scholarship. "Basketball was my passion. I played football not with the intention of going pro. It was just to graduate and make my mom happy." He was just a bigger fan of playing point guard on the basketball court than defense on the pylon. That, and at his comparatively small size (he was 5'10", 225lbs.), he didn't think he was big enough for the NFL.

Everything changed just before Fletcher's senior year in college. His linebacker coach, coincidentally, had also coached the late all-pro linebacker Sam Mills, who was 5'9" and 230lbs. After reading an article about Mills, Fletcher realized how similar they were. Here was a relatively small guy who attended a Division III college and excelled—Mills still holds three Montclair State University tackling records—then was undrafted and ultimately cut by the Cleveland Browns. He went on to play phenomenal defense in the short-lived United States Football League before transitioning to the NFL in 1986, via the Saints.

"That was my outlier moment. After that, I knew I could play well at that level, and I got focused. I had a great senior season because my linebacker coach knew how to use a smaller guy. I wasn't the biggest guy on the field, but I had technique, and I played well. I learned to use what we called the 'hat-in-hands' defense—hitting with the crown of my helmet and my hands at once. I instinctively wanted to make every tackle."

This same consistency followed him into retirement and can now be seen in his commitment to his family, his job as a studio analyst for the CBS Sports Network TV show *TOPS*, and the work of his foundation, London's Bridge, which he set up in 2003. The foundation, which provides college preparatory opportunities for inner-city children, allows him to put his sociology degree to use, as well as what he's learned from being a pro football player.

"Sociology is all about dealing with people, and understanding how to deal in relationships. Football is easy; it's actually the easiest thing I've ever done in my life. Football teaches you so much, from a character standpoint. It taught me how to lead, and how to sacrifice too. When to speak, when to listen, and when to encourage people."

He is most encouraged today by sustaining a strong and happy relationship with his wife and three children, to whom he feels he owes the most time. Even though he spends the week studying film from football games and prepping for the taping of *TOPS* on weekends, he's right back on a plane every Sunday so he can focus on his family. "I know they suffered. I was consumed with football when I was playing; even on vacations I wasn't always engaged mentally.

Now, with a job that allows him to stay close to football, a schedule that gives him time to reconnect with loved ones, and a grounded sense of purpose and spirituality through his charitable works and Christian faith, he looks forward to all that comes after the game ends and life begins.

"I don't miss the game…a ton. I'm blessed to have my family and my career, and I love what I do. I just never wanted to cheat the game, I never wanted to cheat my employer, and I never wanted to cheat myself, or my teammates."

You could say that's for the record.

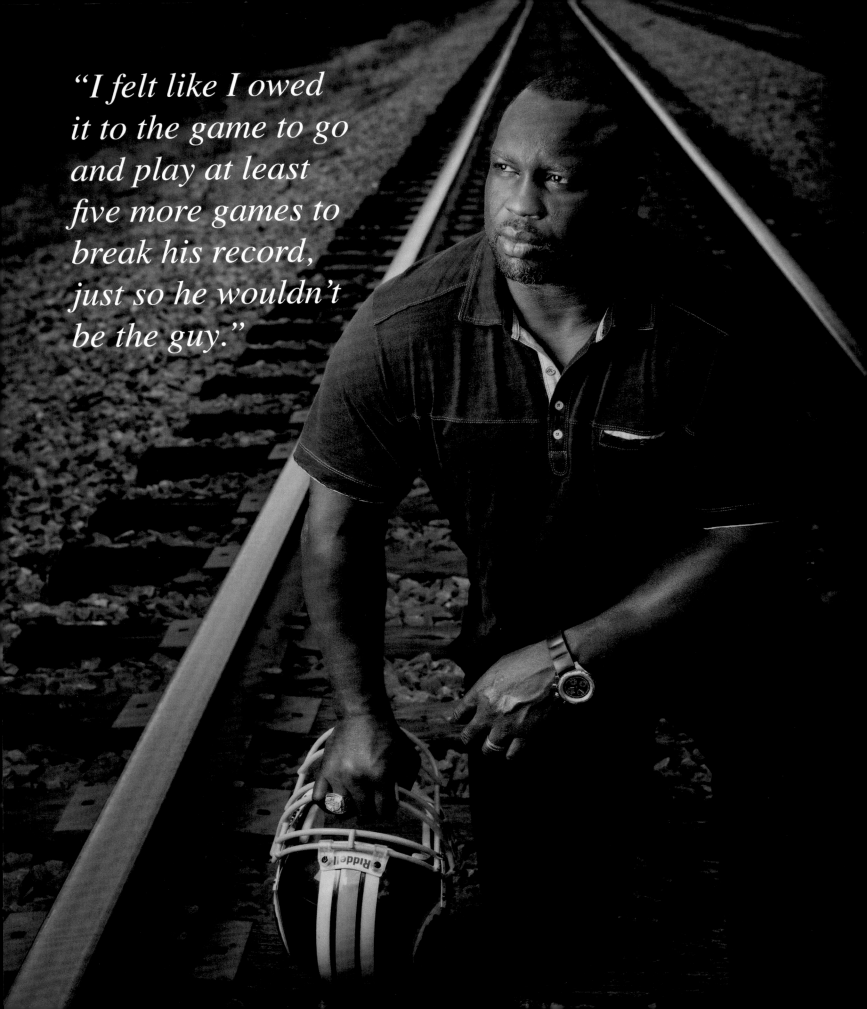

"I felt like I owed
it to the game to go
and play at least
five more games to
break his record,
just so he wouldn't
be the guy."

KEVIN GREENE
NO. **91**

BORN: SCHENECTADY, NEW YORK
COLLEGE: AUBURN UNIVERSITY

NFL CAREER: 15 SEASONS
NFL TEAM: LOS ANGELES RAMS (1985-1992), PITTSBURGH STEELERS (1993-1995)
CAROLINA PANTHERS (1996) SAN FRANCISCO 49ERS (1997)
CAROLINA PANTHERS (1998-1999)
HALL OF FAME INDUCTION: 2016

CAREER HIGHLIGHTS AND AWARDS
5× PRO BOWL (1989, 1994–1996, 1998)
3× FIRST-TEAM ALL-PRO (1989, 1994, 1996)
NFL 1990S ALL-DECADE TEAM
1996 NEA NFL DEFENSIVE PLAYER OF THE YEAR
1996 UPI NFC DEFENSIVE PLAYER OF THE YEAR
1996 NFL ALUMNI NFL LINEBACKER OF THE YEAR
1998 NFLPA NFC LINEBACKER OF THE YEAR
1996 NFLPA NFC LINEBACKER OF THE YEAR
1994 NFLPA AFC LINEBACKER OF THE YEAR
AFC CHAMPION (1995)
THIRD MOST CAREER SACKS IN NFL HISTORY
RECORD 160 SACKS BY A LINEBACKER
OLDEST PLAYER TO LEAD AN NFL SEASON IN SACKS (1996, AGE 34, 14.5 SACKS)
MOST DOUBLE DIGIT SACK SEASONS 34 YEARS OLD AND BEYOND (4).
PRO FOOTBALL HALL OF FAME INDUCTEE (2016)

AS COACH
SUPER BOWL CHAMPION (XLV)

"You may get me one time, you may even get me another. But at the end of the day, I will kick your ass on a physical level that you have not yet known. I will not blink. Just know that. That is my resolve."

Kevin Greene believes everyone has choices to make. Some choices are harder to make than others, and some require a level of fortified resolve that not every person has, or at least has not yet discovered or developed. At several points in his life and career, Greene has found himself at personal crossroads that required very real choices about who he was, and what he was willing to invest and endure, to achieve his goals. Standing firmly upon these decisions, Greene says, is what molded and developed him into the famously fearsome individual known today as one of pro football's all-time greatest defensive players.

"Hitting someone hard is really a mental decision you make—that's what I feel. I feel that in order to hit someone harder than he's gonna hit you, you have to mentally make a decision. You have to say, 'No matter what size you are, no matter what color you are, no matter how hard you are, I am going to kick your ass.'"

He's kicked quite a few. "I tackled quarterbacks from around the corner, with a full head of steam and significant strength. I did not slow down; I ran through them, and they were not expecting it." He's also quite comfortable naming his victims, many of whom rank among the NFL's most famous players. "The John Elways, the Joe Montanas of the world," Green affirms. "Brett Favre. I caught him one time…planted him like a tulip. I'm not even sure he saw it. I hit him as hard as I humanly, possibly could, and it really felt great. Now they would kick my ass out of the League if I hit somebody, in present day NFL, as I hit those guys."

For his part, Greene is proud. He certainly shows no signs of being haunted by his greatest and hardest hits. "You have to decide. Am I gonna be soft or am I gonna be hard? Am I gonna be the hardest of the hard? You have to just set your jaw and go with it."

Greene's own jaw was set early. He credits his upbringing to lessons learned from his father, an airborne ranger in the U.S. Army, who Greene calls "a true, professional soldier." Since his birth in Schenectady, New York, in 1962, Greene and his family moved every three years, according to military assignments. They spent six years living in Germany, from Munich to Mannheim, and were stationed in military housing at Benjamin Franklin Village, where they were surrounded by multicultural military families. Greene calls the Army "a melting pot for all shapes, forms, nationalities, colors, and creeds." He played football for the AYA, or Athletic Youth Association, and recalls his time on base as a beginning—the time he started to become a great linebacker. From ages 10 to 12, he was competing against incredibly gifted players.

The head coach of Greene's AYA team was his father, and Greene remembers being matched up against his older brother, who he says was tougher, harder, and more physical. "He would match us up, one-on-one like an Oklahoma drill, to show everyone else how it's done. We'd lay on our backs, pointing toward each other with about three or four yards between us. He'd blow the whistle, and we'd get up and charge head-on at each other to see who would knock the other on his back. He'd give us 15 reps. I was literally crying, but it made me want more, because I knew my brother was tougher. That's when I started turning hard."

Moving to Granite City was fairly uneventful, as his high school was better known for its soccer team, which won back-to-back-to-back state championships, than for its football team. He only played during his junior and senior years and says they were fairly unremarkable. With no big-time scholarship offers on the radar, he moved to Anniston, Alabama, to attend Auburn University, enlisting in basic training at Fort McClellan along the way. When he finished training, he decided to try playing for Auburn as a walk-on.

"The second game of the season had already been played, but I walked on anyway. I wanted to be part of Auburn. And I'd just come out of three months of basic training, lean and mean, weighing two hundred pounds. I just got done running five miles before breakfast, digging potholes, throwing hand grenades, and shooting machine guns. But after about two weeks I realized I could not compete with these kids. These guys were big, strong, fast, and I was out.

Green walked off the team and was commissioned as second lieutenant in the Army Reserve. Still, he couldn't give up on wearing a Tigers jersey and helmet. "I started working out and would watch Auburn play, peeking through fence. Over the years I sat out, I gained 25 pounds. I could actually strike back with some weight and power. In January 1983, the winter quarter of my third year at Auburn, I went and walked back on, knowing I only had a quarter of my junior year and my senior year. And I knew I'd be punching out, being in the Army and flying around in helicopters. But I walked back on with a much better performance. I wanted to get on that team, to wear that jersey, and to have the sun on my face in Jordan-Hare Stadium."

In 1983, Green was awarded Most Improved Defensive Linebacker. "The first year I played was my senior year. My fourth year of school. They bestowed the award on me, and I was like, 'Yeah, this is fun!'" He remembers the feeling of playing against teams he'd always dreamed of meeting on the field—Georgia, Florida, and of course Alabama. "I came back for a 5th year, my second senior year, and Coach [Pat Dye] started me. Before I could blink, I had eleven sacks that year. I figured, 'Wow, that's kinda cool.… That's productive. Maybe—maybe—if this thing goes well, I can walk on some other place.' I asked Coach Dye. He said, 'I believe there is a place for you in the NFL, and I believe you'll find it.' That's exactly what I wanted to hear." Greene says after that conversation with Pat Dye, he set his mind. "Whether I got drafted or not, I was going to knock on somebody's door and say, 'Let me show you what a guy like me can do. I may be limited athletically, but I can hit somebody. Hard.'"

He was drafted by the Los Angeles Rams in 1985 and says he did "some good things on defense. I got better as a linebacker, more productive. Everybody looked at L.T. [Lawrence Taylor] as the prototypical linebacker. I was cast in his mold, but obviously I wanted to be better than him. I was able to do that. In fifteen years." (Greene broke L.T.'s record for most sacks by a linebacker in 1997 and currently has the third most sacks of any linebacker in NFL history.)

He says he really developed the techniques and fundamentals through experimentation. "I think the 3–4 defense was very young when L.T. and Rickey Jackson were playing well, and I'm not sure there were a lot of coaches who knew how to coach this position that L.T. kinda created—the physical, punishing, 'Terminator of the Gridiron' position. But I learned a lot of things that made me successful on the field through trial and error, and I was always good at taking notes. I was being a true pro. In a lot of cases I created techniques because they really helped me, and no coach could show them to me."

This came in handy when he was called on by the Green Bay Packers to become an outside linebacker coach in 2009. "I basically taught those kids the same things that worked for me—everything that helped me defeat anybody that tried to block me and helped me get a hundred sixty sacks in my career. I knew that if the kids listened to me, I could show them exactly how to defeat the block, because I lived it. I would show them highlight clips of me doing a specific fundamental, like the pass rush. They watched how I dropped players. 'Look at my aiming point. Look where my eyes are. Where are my hands? Where are my strike points? Where am I hitting the offensive tackle?' I would tell them, 'Do exactly what I want you to do, and you'll have a high level of success.' Then I'd say, 'Now, let's go out on the field, and let me show you exactly what you just saw me do on the tape.' I would take Clay Matthews and all my kids. 'This is step one. Step two. Step three.' I was able to break down my process and show kids how I did it. They learned it, and then they could replicate. And consequently, they had, or continue to have, fine careers. It works. And if you have athletic ability, it works even more."

Now, at 53 years old, Greene has stepped away from coaching in the NFL. He says it may be temporary but insists that he left for a great reason: to pour his energy into his son, Gavin, who, much like his father in his younger days, is just over six feet tall, weighs 200 pounds, and plays outside linebacker.

"I basically stepped away from Green Bay because I couldn't justify pouring myself into Clay, Andy [Mulumba], Nate [Palmer], Mike [Neal], and those kids, and teaching them all tricks of the trade, when I have a son in high school trying to play the same position as Dad...getting the eye of the tiger, saying, 'Show me, dad!' So that's what I did. I stepped away. Five years was enough at that point."

Now, with the blessing of his son's head coach, Green is coaching Gavin and six other defensive linebackers at Niceville High School in the Florida Panhandle, and he says he's having the time of his life. "I'm teaching them some really next-level shit, the same shit I taught Clay and my guys at Green Bay. Techniques and fundamentals that made those guys pretty good. I'm seeing my son and all the kids respond to the things I'm teaching them. They're sponges; they want to learn. 'Gimme more! I wanna know what you know, because you were very successful. Show me!' It's really, really cool."

As Gavin graduates and move on, Greene is hopeful that colleges will look at him and has understandably high hopes for his son. While he hasn't ruled out returning to a coaching position in the NFL ("Maybe next year...I don't know. I had a great time and a lot of fun, but I'm having a lot of fun this year at the high school level, so obviously it's not about the money."), he has other dreams he'd like to see come to fruition, and for now he's made up his mind to give them a chance at reality. He admits he enjoys coaching Gavin so much that he's toying with the idea of Gavin attending Auburn and the possibility of being able to coach his son at his alma mater. That, he says, would be the greatest thing he could imagine – worth every hard choice he's made, and worth more than anything he's ever accomplished.

"He's gonna be like me," Greene says. "The last two games, he's been Player of the Game at his high school, so he's smelling the proverbial blood in the water. He has the hunter's heart, and he's going to have the biggest heart of anybody on his team. He's never gonna stop or blink."

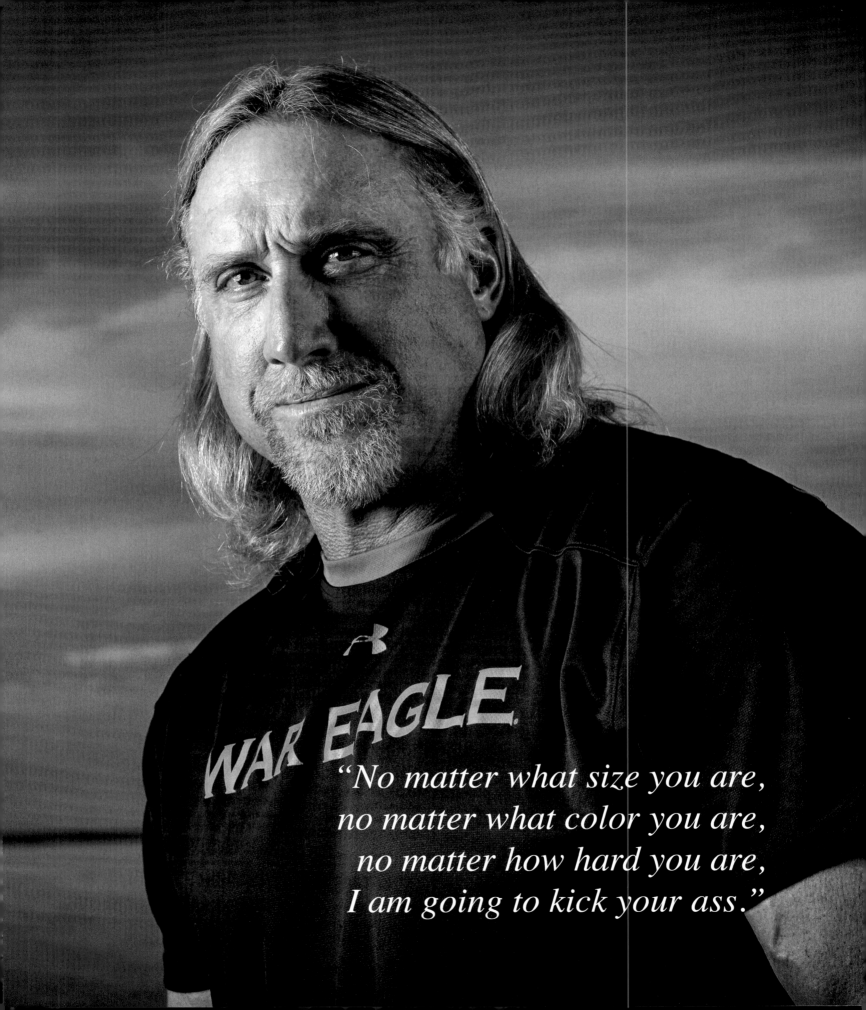

"No matter what size you are,
no matter what color you are,
no matter how hard you are,
I am going to kick your ass."

TED HENDRICKS
NO.**83**

BORN: GUATEMALA CITY, GUATEMALA

COLLEGE: UNIVERSITY OF MIAMI

NFL CAREER: 15 SEASONS

NFL TEAM: BALTIMORE COLTS (1969-1973), GREEN BAY PACKERS (1974)

OAKLAND RAIDERS (1975-1981) LOS ANGELES RAIDERS (1982-1983)

HALL OF FAME INDUCTION: 1990

CAREER HIGHLIGHTS AND AWARDS

4× SUPER BOWL CHAMPION (V, XI, XV, XVIII)

8× PRO BOWL (1971–1974, 1980–1983)

4× FIRST-TEAM ALL-PRO (1971, 1974, 1980, 1982)

5× SECOND-TEAM ALL-PRO (1972, 1973, 1976–1978)

7× FIRST-TEAM ALL-CONFERENCE (1971, 1972, 1974, 1976, 1980–1982)

3× SECOND-TEAM ALL-CONFERENCE (1973, 1978, 1983)

NFL 75TH ANNIVERSARY ALL-TIME TEAM

NFL 1970S ALL-DECADE TEAM

20/20 CLUB

2× FIRST-TEAM ALL-AMERICAN (1967, 1968)

SECOND-TEAM ALL-AMERICA (1966)

UPI LINEMAN OF THE YEAR (1968)

RANKED #82 PLAYER OF ALL-TIME BY NFL NETWORK

PRO FOOTBALL HALL OF FAME (1990)

COLLEGE FOOTBALL HALL OF FAME (1987)

"A Renaissance Man"

Hall-of-Famer Ted Hendricks has never asked for a lot of attention – not even when he was in his prime as an NFL linebacker taking apart offensive teams every week. Certainly not even when playing through significant injuries every week. Getting bruised up a bit was, in Hendricks' mind, something to be tolerated and added to his expectations of what had to be done to arrive at the point of victory.

"You had to sacrifice your body. I had a bunch of broken thumbs and fingers. A bunch of groin muscles pulled. I remember I'd separated ribs against Buffalo. I also remember the two torn groin muscles I had my last year – they were the most painful. They would tape me up and send me back in the game. I have a high pain tolerance; you get in shape and you get used to it. I figured I wasn't hindering anybody because I was still playing. I guess it was the love of the game, because I never wanted to come out and never missed a game. You couldn't keep me off the field."

To be sure there were what Hendricks calls "big load" running backs, fullbacks, and other players he thought twice about tackling back when he played for the Baltimore Colts, Green Bay Packers, and the Oakland Raiders. "Pete Johnson, from the Bengals, Earl Campbell with his big thighs, and Walter Payton, who was like a jackrabbit. You knew you were going to stress your muscles out. I had to tell myself to get ready for punishment."

"The amount of hits you give and take playing professional football when I did take a toll on your body." In explaining how he consistently performed at such a high level, again and again, Hendricks uses plain talk and credits the study and practice of his craft with sharpening his mind and body for championship level play. You see, Ted is not a natural trash-talker. He had a stealthy and cerebral presence on the field that led to his collection of four Super Bowl rings. Both Don Shula and John Madden have remarked he is the smartest player they ever coached.

"I guess you might say I was a durable guy, and had a little intelligence, too. I studied the game. Some said I had a photographic memory. Perhaps my physics background helped. I'd just study the theories, plans, and tendencies. The game just made sense to me. Talent gets you only so far. You gotta study all phases of the game to have an advantage."

Hendricks comes from modest family roots originating in his birth country of Guatemala to being the paperboy for 350 homes in Miami Springs, Florida. He learned about hard work, responsibility, and how to love the sports of both of his countries, as he spent each vacation playing soccer with his cousins in his native Guatemala, then playing baseball and basketball with his block of friends in Miami. He didn't get started on football until his still-developing frame caught up with the challenges of the tall but skinny guy being "over weight" for the optimist club team.

"I was over weight because of my height. One year I was 115 pounds, and I was 140 the next year."
He remembers how he would tower over his friends on the pitching mound and basketball court but was unable to play football. Things changed while attending Hialeah High School. There were no weight restrictions so he participated in four sports every year.

He wouldn't have much more luck putting on pounds playing at the University of Miami, first as a tight end who still holds receiving records for The U and then as a defensive lineman with the nickname, "The Mad Stork," which was bestowed upon him due to his height, arm span, and willingness to get after the ball. A fifth-place Heisman finalist, he was named All-American for three years and still holds the record for most defensive tackles of any Miami football player. Even with such dominant athletic gifts and his awareness of the game, Hendricks is reluctant to give himself too much credit. "The competition of the game kept bringing me back. And the team. I depended on people to do their jobs and helped them out any way I could. I kept telling everybody the ball is the most important thing.

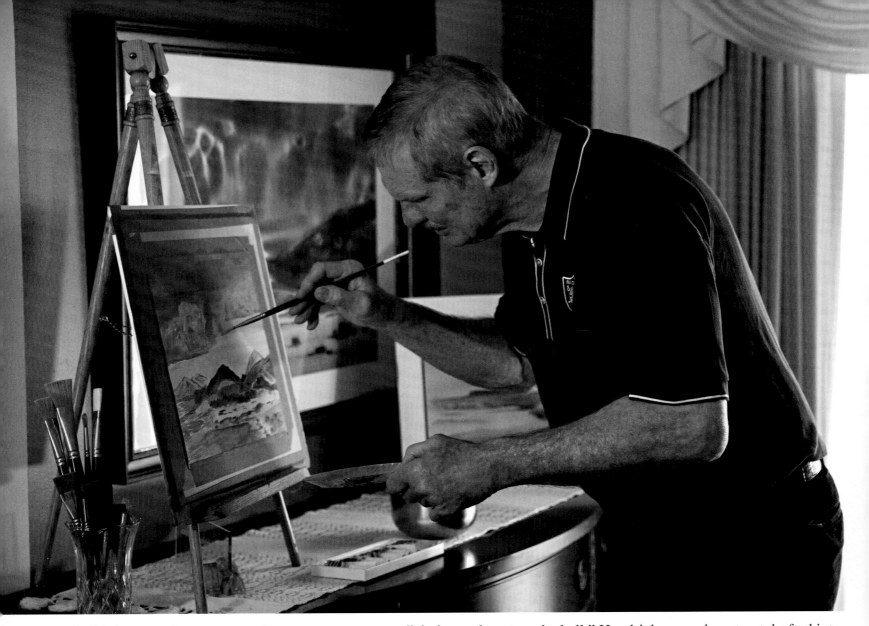

It didn't matter how many sacks you got; you try to dislodge and capture the ball." Hendricks was almost not drafted into the NFL. He was told he was too tall and too skinny at 6'7" and 195 pounds. The then-Baltimore Colts took a chance on him and, "At training table, Coach Shula would put extra potatoes and ice cream in front of me to make me gain weight. It didn't do any good." He says he was never a fan of weightlifting, but he would always try to be in the front with wind sprints and conditioning. "It was just determination to be as good as I could possibly be. With practice you refine things like that. Usually I had backs blocking me that were smaller than me, but I was basically practicing every day, knowing and anticipating what they were going to do, and getting better at it."

Hendricks went from good to great through his willingness to learn from, and be open to, the wisdom and training of great players and coaches like John Unitas and Don Shula who directed the Colts in the '60s. "John would mess with my head and make me learn everything about the offense and Shula was a perfectionist. With Shula, we had to run a mile in under six minutes before we even started training camp. And that's when training camp was six weeks and two-a-days. He's one of the coaches who made you get back on track to play as a unit."

Such lessons came in handy at pivotal points in Hendricks' career. He specifically remembers the firing of Don McCafferty, the Baltimore offensive coordinator who took over as the Colts' head coach and led them to win the Super Bowl when Don Shula left for the Dolphins and the next game after the firing.

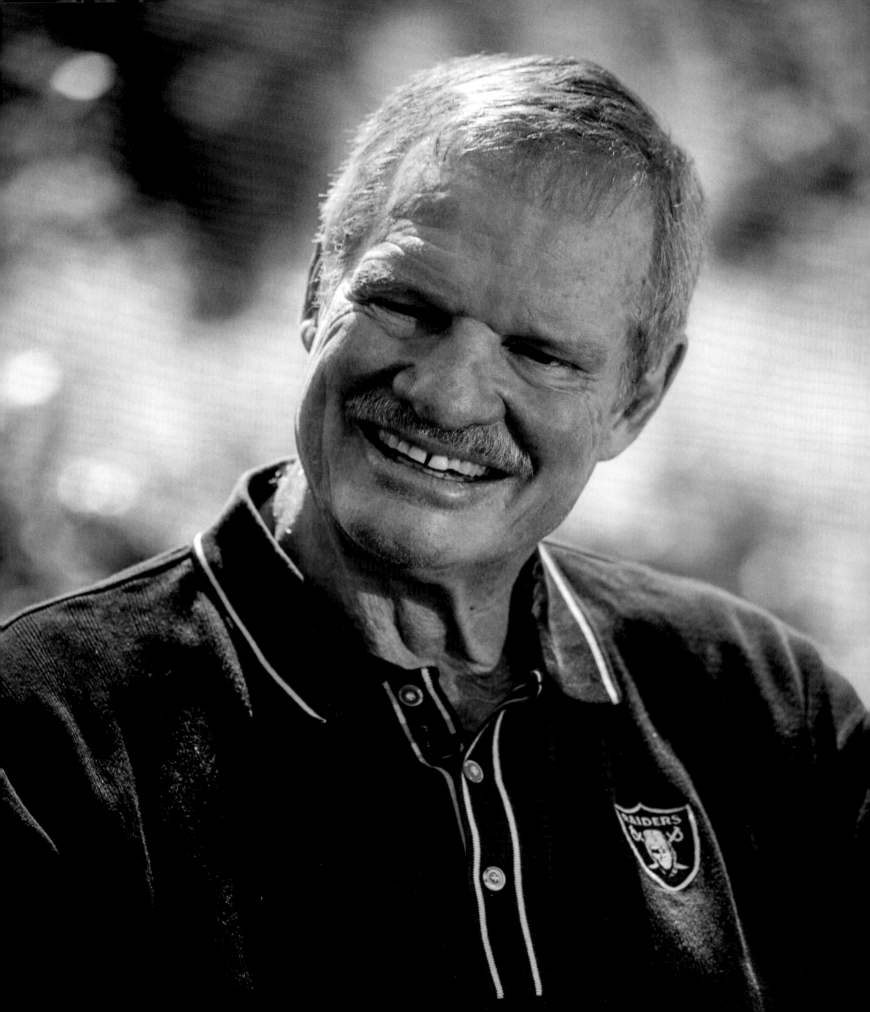

"That was really tough. Everybody loved him," Hendricks remembers. "Before the game started we weren't even gonna play, but we got talked into it, for the sake of the assistant coaches. That was one of the occasions of tough decisions, although a lot of them I didn't have any control over, so there wasn't any use getting upset about it. No grudges; it's all part of the game. You played full steam, and if they beat you, you remembered it, and you were ready the next time."

"Preparation was a lot," he says of his football education, "but finding out how your opponents looked in films earlier in the week and studying their habits makes it work out a lot better, because there were a lot of guys faster than me. When things weren't going so well, and you lost a couple of games, you had to bear down and work harder at it."

He watched and learned from other players at his position, including All-Pro Colts middle linebacker Mike Curtis, who used his height as an advantage and would reach over to grab his opponents. Curtis was not only known for hitting players, but also one infamous fan, hard. "Blew him up," Hendricks says with a laugh, and recalls another time when Baltimore played Green Bay, and Curtis clotheslined Jim Grabowski so hard his helmet flew off. "Afterward, I picked it up and gave it back to Jim, and said, 'Here, take it. And you're going the wrong way.' I thought he had knocked his head off at first."

There were also times he didn't always find it so funny on the field when things became dangerous. He never found it funny when overzealous players played outside the rules and may have jeopardized an opponent's career. That's not his style.

Hendricks was traded to Green Bay in 1974, and might have been stuck there if not for contractual circumstances that worked out in his favor, such as being traded by Baltimore, and becoming a free agent after spending his option year as a Packer. Though he'd signed a future contract to play for the World Football League, it dissolved, leaving Hendricks free to sign a new contract with the Oakland Raiders, where he would play under John Madden and Tom Flores and win three more Super Bowl rings.

Today, Hendricks lives near Chicago, enjoying great food, the "almost country" atmosphere, studying history and honing his skills as a painter. Ted is directly involved with the Ted Hendricks Award, which annually recognizes the best defensive end in collegiate football, and managing his charitable Ted Hendricks Foundation, whose mission is providing assistance to programs benefiting health, educational and recreational programs for both youth and seniors. He finds being in the Midwest not only friendly but convenient to reach both Oakland and Miami so he can support his Miami Hurricanes and beloved Raiders whenever possible. He follows college and NFL games and is still a fan of today's players, although he admits to being amazed at how much bigger and faster they are than he and others were back then.

Ted Hendricks continues to approach life as the humble guy from Guatemala and Miami: a Renaissance man now comfortable with everything from black hole theory, classical Greek and Mayan history to the non-contact challenges of oil and watercolor landscapes, while helping others reach their potential.

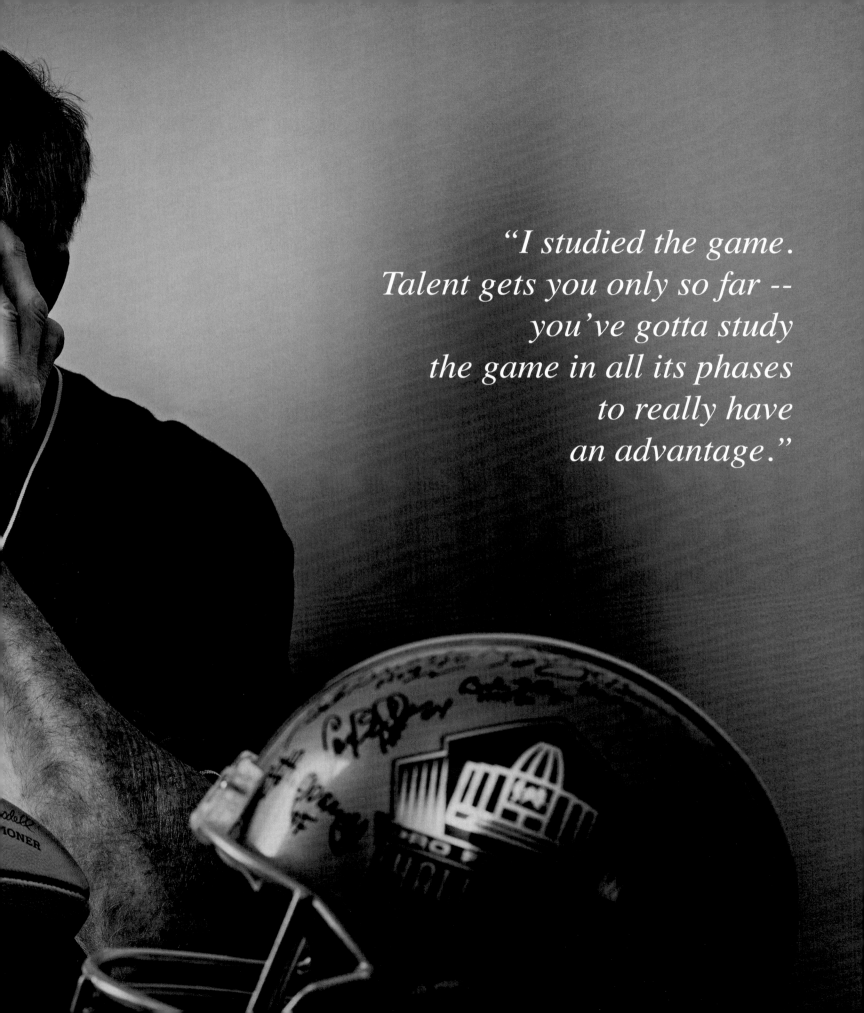

"I studied the game.
Talent gets you only so far --
you've gotta study
the game in all its phases
to really have
an advantage."

RICKEY JACKSON
NO.**57**

BORN: PAHOKEE, FLORIDA
COLLEGE: UNIVERSITY OF PITTSBURGH

NFL CAREER: 15 SEASONS
NFL TEAM: NEW ORLEANS SAINTS (1981-1993),
SAN FRANCISCO 49ERS (1994-1995)
HALL OF FAME INDUCTION: 1990

CAREER HIGHLIGHTS AND AWARDS
SUPER BOWL CHAMPION (XXIX)
6× PRO BOWL (1983–1986, 1992, 1993)
4× FIRST-TEAM ALL-PRO (1986, 1987, 1992, 1993)
2× SECOND-TEAM ALL-PRO (1984, 1985)
NFC CHAMPION (1994)
SECOND-TEAM ALL-AMERICAN (1980)

"They have one Hall of Fame Football Player from the Muck. That's me."

Rickey Jackson started playing football at around at 10 years old and remembers being an immediate standout thanks to natural skill and size advantages. As he got older, his abilities put him noticeably beyond others in his age range and above. By the time he hit sixth grade, he was playing against eighth and ninth graders. "People always said how great I was of an athlete. I put licks on players that let everybody around know how good I was. I'd have people coming from all over to see me hit people, from day one."

Jackson's hometown of Pahokee, Florida—nicknamed the Muck—played a major part in motivating him to pursue a career in sports. To this day, Pahokee, population 7,000, seems to grow NFL players as naturally as it grows citrus fruit. More than a dozen natives of this swampy, mineral-rich West Palm Beach town have played professional football, including Jackson, wide receiver Anquan Boldin, and the late Andre Waters.

Maybe it was something in the soil that gave Jackson the drive and determination to succeed at being something other than a migrant farmer. (Pahokee already had plenty.) As geography and genetics would have it, Pahokee was becoming known for breeding kids with football in their bloodstreams. Still, the Muck was also a place that made him aware of reality and gave him the mental and physical hardness he and the other young black men known as the Muck Boys used to become legendary players.

"You had to be tough in that kind of environment," Jackson says. "That was my ticket to get out. I kept from doing a lot of bad things because I knew I had my hometown on my shoulders. A lot of guys played and tried to make it from where I came from."

One standout memory Jackson credits for pushing him forward was a street sign formerly posted at the edge of Pahokee city limits. "Welcome to the home of Mel Tillis," he says, saying it as if he's still reading the words from the now-removed sign. To Jackson, the sign did not reflect the town as a whole. He was always bothered by the implication that Pahokee was only proud of the country singer, who wasn't really even from the city. "He was the only guy on that sign," Jackson says, referring to Tillis, "but look at all the other football players from the same town and high school." By ignoring the dreams he and other Muck Boys had, the sign failed to inspire anyone who wasn't already a Mel Tillis fan.

Jackson's name is now on a Pahokee road sign posted in honor of his NFL Hall of Fame membership, and the city is proud of its hometown hero. He continues to feel an obligation to inspire young men who may earn the right one day to have their own names honored, and he hopes that his accomplishments are an example of possibilities beyond the Muck.

"I tried then, and I try now, to make sure I keep the light shining. It lets all these young guys know that they can make it. When I was growing up, we had a town full of a mix of people, white and black. White people ran the town, ran everything. Now it's probably 90 percent black, five percent white, and the rest Hispanic. The mayor and five city commissioners are now black. The whole town changed. But back then, I tried hard to make sure I made it. I had to push. I had a reason."

His reason was knowing he deserved an opportunity, even when he was being overlooked. As a high school tight end at Pahokee High School, Jackson willed himself into the Florida High School Athletic Association's All-Century Team, becoming one of the best 33 students in the history of high school football in the state, with 188 tackles and 21 pass receptions, including eight touchdowns.

He attended college at the University of Pittsburgh, playing with quarterback Dan Marino, and alongside linebacker and College Football Hall of Famer Hugh Green. While it would have been easy to be overshadowed by the two, his 290 tackles certainly contributed to the team's victorious season. Still, Jackson felt overlooked, especially after being the 53rd overall pick in the second round of the NFL Draft. So again, he found himself with something to prove.

"All of them were good," Jackson admits when remembering all the players drafted before him, including Green, Ronnie Lott, and Lawrence Taylor. "But my position, the side I played, I felt like they couldn't play. I knew I had a great skill from God, so I didn't worry about much."

In fact, Jackson worried so little that by the time he retired from the NFL in 1995, he'd made six Pro Bowl appearances, risen to third place all-time among NFL sack leaders, been an All-Pro six times, and earned a Super Bowl championship ring with the San Francisco 49ers in his final year playing pro football—the only year he did not play for the New Orleans Saints.

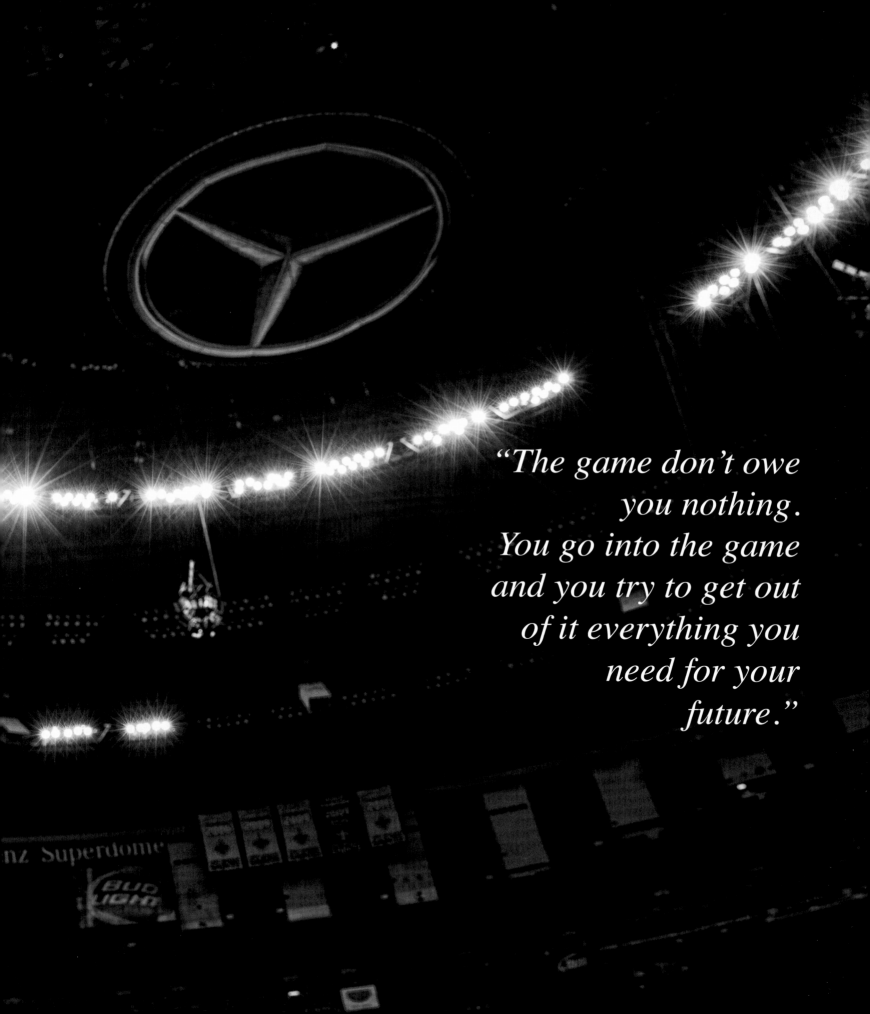

"The game don't owe
you nothing.
You go into the game
and you try to get out
of it everything you
need for your
future."

He calls great linebackers like Jack Ham and Robert "Dr. Doom" Brazile his own inspirations. "I always wanted to be like those guys. They wanted the ball, and they wanted the guy with the ball. Those two, they played the game smart. They didn't worry about hitting anybody that didn't have the ball. I played the same—I always made sure to only worry about where the football was. I wanted the ball, and everybody knew it. The quarterbacks, a lot of times, would throw the ball away so I wouldn't come after them."

"The only time I'd worry about something other than the ball was when I battled against [St. Louis Rams offensive tackle] Jackie Slater. I knew that he knew when he went against me, he was going against the best, and I was gonna bring the fight to him. My whole point was to beat him physically just to show him I was more tough and more man. Otherwise I wasn't concerned. But I hated our division. I was one of the old school guys. We didn't want anything to do with you. If you were in our division, I was trying to kill you."

Jackson sees the league as an entirely different organization now that he's out. "It's more flag football now. Football is at the point now where the guys making all the money have nothing to do with the game, and will never have anything to do with the game. Even with the Tom Brady ruling, if that was anybody's fault, it's the ref's. The referee is responsible for the football. It should have never been on Tom Brady if for every play, the referee got the football and put it down on the field...I didn't understand that. It's just so different now."

He even wades into the controversy surrounding head injuries and the lawsuits that have brought plenty of negative attention to the League. "The lawyers make all the money off concussions. They make sure those guys don't get the concussions we got, and they won't be able to sue like we did. Football players are going to do whatever they can to block each other, just like on the field. They don't stick together. Some of the guys have been hit in the head so much they can't see the big picture. That's why I like baseball. When they get finished, all those guys are in better shape than football players. We amounted to jocks, and we let them get away with it. That's the only thing I hate. I heard some guys are trying to talk to the rookies now, but most of them talking to the rookies ain't never been through nothing, and they're telling rookies what they should do. It lets me know that players still don't get it. But at least there's more money out there for the players than ever. Some of the guys are getting 15 to 20 million dollars. You like that. But everybody ain't getting it. That's something they need to spread around to all 53 guys."

Jackson paid attention to the up-close-and-personal financial lessons he learned as an NFL player, and he now pays himself via his Mr. Saints Petroleum Company of Metairie, which sells diesel, gasoline, and oil to firms, gas stations, and homeowners. He also has a local radio program that airs every Monday, makes appearances on behalf of Budweiser at football events around Louisiana, and enjoys golf when time allows.

For providing opportunities to disadvantaged youth, he was honored with the NFL's Ed Block Courage Award by fellow teammates in 1990, and his name adorns the Rickey Jackson and Friends Community Hope Center, also known as the New Orleans Saints Courage House. The facility offers educational enrichment, career development, counseling, and mentoring, in addition to a computer lab and a recording studio donated by New Orleans-born rap superstar Lil Wayne. "We have a good place over there," he says. "It's good for the kids that come. When they graduate, we give them a thousand dollars as a scholarship. We at least make sure they eat."

And while he's still trying to provide inspiration to the Muck, saying he wants to work with the city of Pahokee to put up a road sign in his hometown honoring every NFL player who came from the city limits, he's also keeping a realist's perspective when it comes to expectations. He believes in hard work, but he's clear on life's lack of guarantees and believes in personal development via commitment to a goal.

"The game don't owe you nothing. You go into the game, and you try to get out of it everything you need for your future."

WILLIE LANIER
NO.**63**

BORN: CLOVER, VIRGINIA

COLLEGE: MORGAN STATE UNIVERSITY

NFL CAREER: 11 SEASONS

NFL TEAM: KANSAS CITY CHIEFS

HALL OF FAME INDUCTION: 1986

*FIRST AFRICAN-AMERICAN MIDDLE LINEBACKER

CAREER HIGHLIGHTS AND AWARDS

2× AFL ALL-STAR GAME (1968, 1969)

6× PRO BOWL (1970–1975)

2× ALL-AFL (1968, 1969)

8× ALL-PRO (1968–1975)

SUPER BOWL CHAMPION (IV)

NFL 75TH ANNIVERSARY ALL-TIME TEAM

NFL MAN OF THE YEAR AWARD (1972)

PRO BOWL CO-MVP (1971)

KANSAS CITY CHIEFS #63 RETIRED

"I never really loved the game."

Willie Lanier strikes one as a truthful man. It's also true that, as a linebacker for the Kansas City Chiefs, he was known for striking some men hard enough to earn the nickname Contact. So it feels strange when the hard-charging former defender says football was never as important to him as it seemed to those watching or playing against him. After all, this is someone who, during his 10-year NFL career, went from a pioneering beginning (he's the first African-American middle linebacker in the League's history) to becoming an All-Star, Pro Bowl MVP, NFL Man of the Year, and Super Bowl champion, and has since not only been named to the Hall of Fame (Pro Football and College) but also been honored by the NFL in 1994 as one of its 75 greatest players of all time.

Today, as a highly successful investor and entrepreneur, Willie Lanier is just as respected for his business acumen as he ever was for his natural physical ability. He became a stockbroker after his retirement from football and went on to sit in the executive seat at several major companies, including a vice-chairmanship at Wells Fargo subsidiary First Union Securities. Born in the small town of Clover, Virginia, Lanier now resides in Midlothian, an historic community not far from where he grew up in Richmond, and runs the investment firm Lanier Group LLC. And aside from being recognized for his achievements, he is as removed from the game as the spectators who once crowded stadiums to see him play, even if he's now watching from the suites instead of the stands.

Like many young men growing up in Richmond (and elsewhere around the U.S.), Lanier got into football simply because friends in his neighborhood played. He was competitive, but only up to a certain point. "I didn't have aggressive tendencies, but I enjoyed participating. At sixteen years of age, my size started to come together, and I went from 150 pounds at fifteen, to 185 to 190 as a sixteen-year old. So then I could play offensive tackle, defensive tackle, whatever. But I still wasn't dominant. I was just a kid who played. It wasn't really based on the love of the game; it was just participating, enjoying the camaraderie, and trying to get better."

Richmond had just two high schools: a vocational school called Armstrong (named for a Union Army general who mentored Booker T. Washington), and Maggie L. Walker, the college preparatory school Lanier attended, which was named for America's first female banker, who happened to be African-American. Lanier describes Walker as a school at which "you would expect to get a different level of education that would allow you to get to college, and hopefully give you a better chance at a longer future. You were expected to achieve something. You were expected to have others know that you were an educated person." Aside from academic influences, he was also learning economics and spending summers in the country with his grandparents, who farmed tobacco. "They were not sharecroppers. They didn't work for somebody to get a piece; they owned it. That meant something relative to my understanding of how everything seemed to work. The framework in our country is that capitalism is what we do; it's what we preach. So to have an astute awareness of capitalism, to be able to understand and talk about it, is to not be viewed as just the employee or the worker, but one who understands a lot more about the whole process. And the only way you can continue to understand that was to be a part of it."

By the time he was a senior at Walker, Lanier weighed 207 pounds—an especially dominant size that set him up for his first season as a linebacker. But with only a year of play to his credit, his only significant scholarship offer came from Virginia State, a college he confesses to being unexcited about attending. "I didn't want to go there because everything was so segregated in Virginia."

He decided to take control of his own future. "I called the coach at Morgan State that July—didn't tell my parents—and told him I wanted to go to his school. He said, 'I don't have any money.' I said, 'I didn't ask you for money; I want to go to your school.'"

"My background
was one of reading,
believing, accepting,
and then being
willing to have
whatever the risk or
challenge."

"The love of my life, from a business standpoint, has always been business."

"So I went up and took the entrance exam, and showed him some film and my transcripts, and was able to score in the top ten percent of the incoming freshman class. He still didn't have any money. I said, 'Well, what will happen is that you'll be so impressed by my academic and athletic work, whatever you need to do after the first semester, you'll do.' And that's how I went to school." He gained another 30 pounds the summer before his freshman year, stepping onto Morgan State's campus at 18 years old standing 6'1" and weighing 245 pounds—the same size he would be when he arrived in the NFL. "God gave me two growth spurts, and it was all there," he recalls.

Thanks to the results of his incoming test at Morgan State, which were obviously boosted by the early education he received at Maggie Walker and his family, Lanier was able to start in an advanced curriculum his freshman year, which he says was more robust than what was available to most entering students. This added to his already confident demeanor, which came about through what he calls "a combination of reading everything that I could, going to church with my parents on Sunday, and seeing how positioning faith in your life gives you an awareness of the ability to challenge many things that can happen. And then just truly believing that the Constitution meant what it meant."

That last bit, Lanier says, is freedom. "How could the desire to have life, liberty, and the pursuit of happiness—how could that benefit you if someone was trying to take it from you? How could you pursue your own? You were confronted by the presumption that you should not speak, that you should not respond to a behavior and action of someone else that abridged your right. For whatever reason, my background was one of reading, believing, accepting, and then being willing to have whatever the risk or challenge."

"The sport was something that, once I understood, I knew how to do it intuitively," Lanier remembers. "I won't call it 'self-taught,' but it's almost that, because I had a lot of trouble listening to coaches. My parents, who were working class African-Americans, had the American Medical Journal in our home. And because I would read it, it gave me the ability to say to coaches when there were things that didn't make sense to me, such as not having any water when it was hot. I'm not gonna do that—I have to be hydrated!"

"I can't imagine being down south with Bear [Bryant] and the Junction City Boys [the Texas A&M Aggies team that Bryant famously— and harshly—trained in 1954], and you're telling me I won't have any water? Guess what I would have done? I gonna get my water, and if you're telling me I can't have my water, I'm just gonna have to leave. Because I am not going to allow you to put me at risk, and my health and future, because you don't seem to understand that which the American Medical Journal said is legitimate from a hydration standpoint."

Lanier insists he wasn't trying to be disrespectful to his coaches but simply wanted to show that he believed in his own intelligence and abilities. "I didn't mind reminding [coaches] that I probably know more than you," he says with a laugh. "I say it like that because things I would try to do were about more than just sport. It was to have a broad breadth of knowledge that I could bring back and tie to the sport. If you understood physics, geometry, leverage…all of those things meant more to me than somebody trying to diagram a play and say, 'You need to go here, then yon.' Because if I understand leverage, if I understand geometry, if I understand all of that, I can get it done in a way that you might not have even thought about—a way that is more applicable to my unique set of skills. That was always very important."

Though Lanier is clearly a confident man, he is also spiritually grounded, using boldness as a tool that would never allow him be too shy to apply his personal and intellectual strengths. "All of us draw from observing others who are able to take a space and move it, regardless of what the odds appear to be. If that can't be what happens for everyone, then we as a democracy are not really who we say we are. So there have to be those sentinels who continue to let that be seen."

"God's given me the ability to give comment on many things extemporaneously. My journey has been one that is very difficult to define me because there is a breadth of activities, knowledge, and interest, that on any particular day it's not easily definable. But it comes from being very confident that, if you're a quick study, I can compete with anybody, anywhere, anytime. And I don't mind a challenge." Lanier says he wants to be remembered as "a highly intelligent African-American male who had the ability to play a sport all the way to the Hall of Fame; to take business situations, no matter how daunting, all the way through to their conclusion; to constantly assist others and let them recognize they can raise their levels always higher. The confidence required to do that is never ending."

So no, it's not often you hear someone who's made it as far in athletics as Lanier admit that, yes, he may have simply been married to the sport for a time, yet his former career was mostly a business arrangement that worked for both parties as long as it could—one that led him to where his heart truly lies. And he doesn't flinch or betray the slightest emotion when he says, "The love of my life, from a business standpoint, has always been business."

Photo by *Julia Brewer /Sports Illustrated/Getty Images*

MIKE SINGLETARY
NO.50

BORN: HOUSTON, TEXAS

COLLEGE: BAYLOR UNIVERSITY

NFL CAREER: 12 SEASONS

NFL TEAM: CHICAGO BEARS (1981-1992)

HALL OF FAME INDUCTION: 1998

CAREER HIGHLIGHTS AND AWARDS

10× PRO BOWL (1983–1992)

8× FIRST-TEAM ALL-PRO (1983–1989, 1991)

SECOND-TEAM ALL-PRO (1990)

SUPER BOWL CHAMPION (XX)

NFL 1980S ALL-DECADE TEAM

2× AP NFL DEFENSIVE PLAYER OF THE YEAR (1985, 1988)

3× UPI NFC PLAYER OF THE YEAR (1984, 1985, 1988)

INDUCTED INTO THE PRO FOOTBALL HALL OF FAME (1998)

COACH:

SAN FRANCISCO / INTERIM HEAD COACH 49ERS (2008)

SAN FRANCISCO 49ERS / **HEAD COACH** (2009–2010)

"Growing up, I did not want to identify with Jesus Christ."

To most football fans familiar with Mike Singletary, this quote might seem highly unlikely. What people may not know is that Singletary, who like Reggie White was also called Minister of Defense by his Chicago Bears teammates, struggled with spirituality and depression in his formative years.

One of the all-time greatest defensive players, Singletary was brought up in a deeply Christian home with nine brothers and sisters, his mother, Rudell and father, Charles, a Pentecostal street preacher who built his own church and played guitar. The tragic deaths of two of his brothers when he was still coming of age naturally caused Singletary to question his understanding of religion and what he was raised to believe. One brother, Dale, died accidentally due to carbon monoxide poisoning from breathing in fumes from a coal stove in their house while sleeping. Another, Grady, who stepped in as a role model after their father left their mother, was killed by a drunk driver.

Singletary also had to deal with the conflicting nature of football in relation to his family's religious beliefs. "Understand that, being the last of 10 kids and my father being a Pentecostal pastor, playing football—and any kind of sport—was against our religion. I was playing football around the neighborhood, but I really wasn't supposed to be playing. None of my family, none of my elder sisters and brothers, ever participated in sports."

Losing Grady, who would show up at all of his seventh grade football games to cheer him on (Singletary's father did not attend), was the moment when Singletary began to drift. "It was a little bit overbearing—kind of over the edge for me. I began to shut down inside. I was pretty much a follower up until that time. Wanting to fit in and wanting to be accepted. After those two events happened, I felt like I wanted to be left alone, to withdraw, to shut down. I'd made a decision that I didn't want to try to be anything special. I didn't want to try to be the best that I could be because it doesn't matter anyway. 'What's gon' happen is gon' happen.'" For reasons also related to apathy, Singletary didn't want to be the worst at anything either, out of fear that no one would want to be associated with him. He aimed for mediocrity until his mother began to notice and told him that he had to change.

"She looked at me and understood my body language, and sat me down to talk to me about the value I brought to the family. There was something special about me, she said, and God had a plan for my life. She asked me to be the man of the house. I wanted to say, 'Mom, I don't want to do that. I'm really getting comfortable, really quickly, with this decision to be mediocre.' But I couldn't tell her that because I realized that she really believed in me. It ended up being one of the greatest conversations I ever had. I got up from the table, walked in my room, and wrote out a mission statement."

Written when he was just 12 years old, that mission statement profoundly defined the man, minister, and professional football icon that Mike Singletary would become. In it, he vowed to obtain a college scholarship and a degree, become an All-American college football player, get drafted to the NFL, become an All-Pro, buy his mother a house and take care of her for the rest of her life, and own his own business. Though he grew up in a poor neighborhood, one that might be described as a ghetto, he was determined from that point on to succeed and has since accomplished everything in that document.

"That became my drive, and I believe it's so important in life that if there's something you want to do, it needs to be written down. That vision statement allowed me to have boundaries because I knew how I was going to get there. And it was by saying no to drugs, no to alcohol, no to the bad crowd; it allowed me to stop being a follower and begin to look at the things that God put inside me. There were seeds of greatness in me. At that particular time and day, the call in my life was realized, and I began to move forward and live that duty. That was really the pride and the passion."

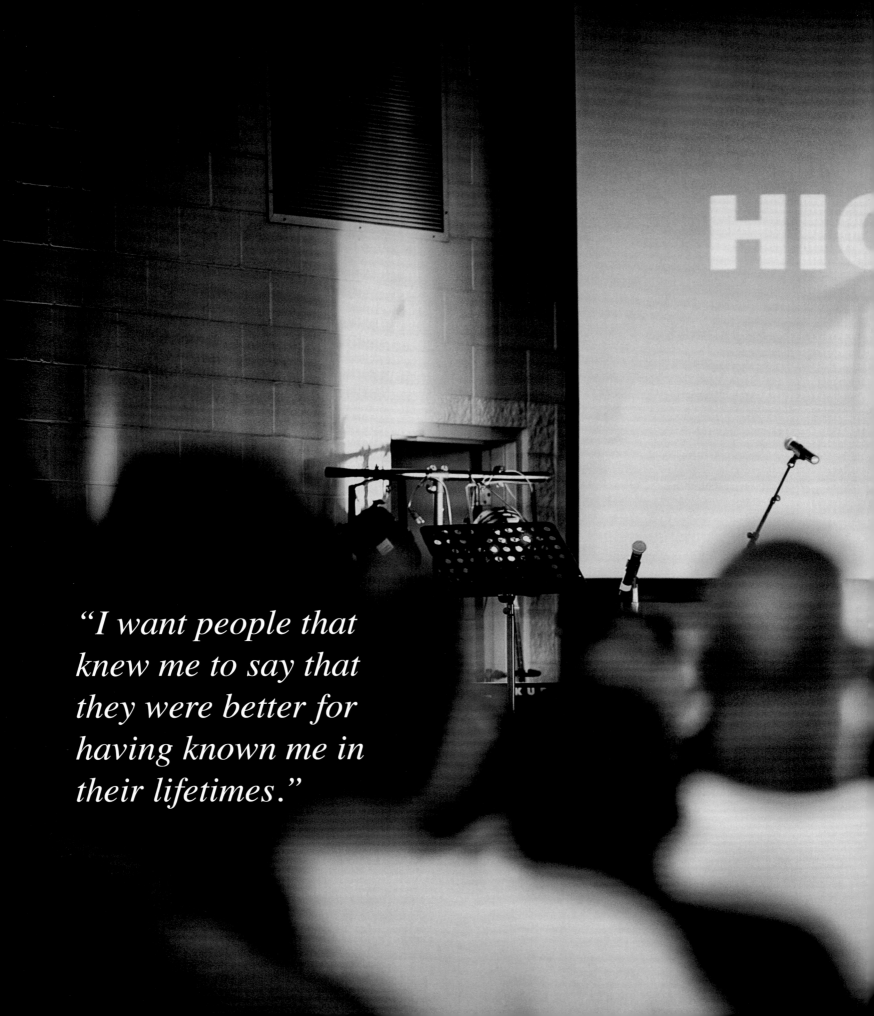

"*I want people that knew me to say that they were better for having known me in their lifetimes.*"

"Those were the times. Sometimes I would just get up at night and go start running. This dream was very much alive in my head, and it allowed me to go the extra mile, go take an extra step, and not allow myself to have pity parties or setbacks or whatever, but to continue to move forward and do the best I could do."

The best Mike Singletary could do was become a force of nature. At Baylor University, he set a school record for making a total of 662 tackles in four years, becoming the only college junior to ever make the All-Southwest Conference team in the 1970s, and going on to be an All-American and recipient of the Davey O'Brien Award for outstanding Southwest players. As a Chicago Bear, he recorded almost 1,500 tackles, missed only two games in his entire 12-year career, was named NFL Defensive Player of the Year in 1985 and 1988, and was elected to the College Football Hall of Fame in 1995 and the Pro Football Hall of Fame three years later. And no one can forget his amazing performance as part of the Bears team that trampled the New England Patriots 46–10 in Super Bowl XX, or his smooth skills on the mic and dance floor as part of the classic "Super Bowl Shuffle" rap song and video.

Singletary's passionate approach to life isn't all-work-and-no-play, as he admits to apparently having moves beyond the line of scrimmage, which he says his wife, Kim and seven children know all too well. "I really love having a good time. I love to dance, to sing. I love music. I dance to all kinds of music. It could be Frank Sinatra, Barry White, Isaac Hayes, Barbra Streisand…it could be anything. I love all types of music, whether it be Christian music or country-western. No one knows that better than my wife and kids. If people knew that about me, it would be crazy; it would really flip 'em out."

Known to teammates as Samurai Mike for his intense focus and hitting ability, Singletary definitely had situations on the field and in the locker rooms that would qualify as flipping out in another sense. As a coach, Singletary admitted to being challenged with "coaching etiquette" for being unafraid to call out his players for delivering sub-par performances. His famous rant against the performance of San Francisco 49ers tight end Vernon Davis, whom he sent off the field during a game against Seattle for what he considered unseemly behavior, is immortalized thanks to YouTube and sports television. Telling reporters in a press conference after losing the game that he'd rather be penalized for having not enough players than to allow one with a bad attitude to influence the team ("Cannot play with 'em. Cannot coach with 'em. Cannot win with 'em. Can't do it!"), Singletary defied contemporary standards. However, Davis has gone on to say that it was Singletary's honesty and mentoring that ultimately made him a better player.

To this point, Singletary does not shy away from his belief that life is about pushing your way through, whether it's against another team's offensive line or against the tribulations of life. He is continuously inspired by the legacies of great people like Martin Luther King, Jr., Gandhi, and or course, Jesus Christ. He also finds that using focused aggression while admiring those who historically stood for nonviolence is completely sensible. "I'm an eye for an eye kind of guy, but the older I've gotten, the more I realize how much strength and courage it takes to turn the other cheek. When I study people that have that inner strength, it gives me strength to recognize that there are only a few up there and out there—you can count 'em on your hands—that are worth their weight in gold, those people that stand for what is right."

So while Singletary may have chosen football because it allowed him to release some of the angst and emotional frustration that came with tragedy in his childhood, it became a statement about the man who has risen to the top of his field and remained humble—at times sporting a coach's cap, at other times wearing a uniform designed to withstand blunt force while battling for victory on the pylon. And he finds peace in learning about others who also stand up and scrap for what they know is a righteous cause.

"I want my life to matter. I want to make a difference. I want my life to count. I want my children to know who I am. I want my wife to feel that she is married to the greatest guy in the world. I want people that knew me to say that they were better for having known me in their lifetimes. Anybody can quit."

"Anybody can give up. I like to hear the stories about the people that did not quit—that found that inner strength. I'm a fighter, and I want to be surrounded by fighters. I try, in my family, to breed fighters. My wife is a fighter, and we fight together. To me that's really what life's all about. It's about giving all you can, and when you think you've given all that you have, you can give some more."

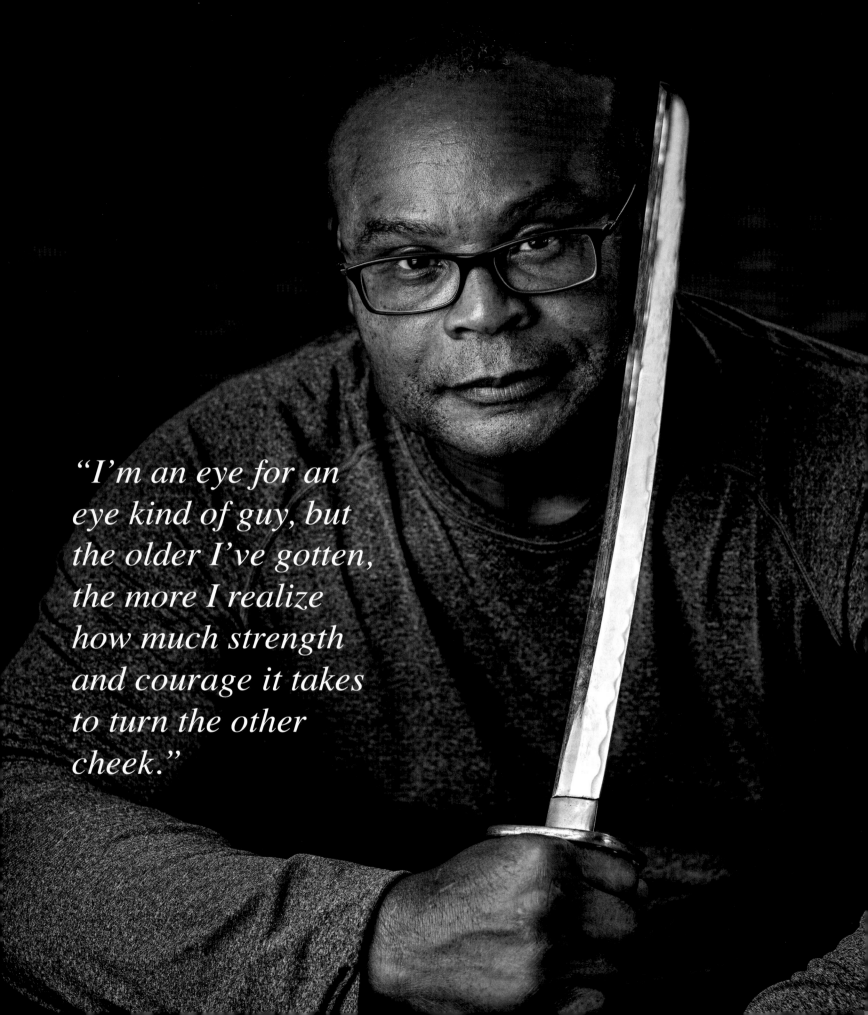

"I'm an eye for an eye kind of guy, but the older I've gotten, the more I realize how much strength and courage it takes to turn the other cheek."

SUPER BOWL
XX
CHAMPIONS

Photo by Rob Tringali/SportsChrome/Getty Images

TAKEO SPIKES
NO.51

BORN: AUGUSTA, GEORGIA

COLLEGE: AUBURN UNIVERSITY

NFL CAREER: 15 SEASONS

NFL TEAM: CINCINNATI BENGALS (1998-2002), BUFFALO BILLS (2003-2006),
PHILADELPHIA EAGLES (2007), SAN FRANCISCO 49ERS (2008-2010),
SAN DIEGO CHARGERS (2011-2012)

CAREER HIGHLIGHTS AND AWARDS

2× PRO BOWL (2003, 2004)

2× ALL-PRO (2003, 2004)

2× PFWA ALL-AFC (2003, 2004)

ED BLOCK COURAGE AWARD (2006)

1996 INDEPENDENCE BOWL MVP

1998 PEACH BOWL MVP

USA TODAY HIGH SCHOOL ALL-AMERICAN (1994)

"Some dream for success. Others wake up and work for it."

CHRIS SHELLING
1994

VICTOR RILEY
1997

KING
89, 1990

ROCKER
1990

TAKEO SPIKES
1997

DAMON DUVAL
2001

"I couldn't care less about American standards."

Don't call Homeland Security - I love my country. I just believe, as one of my favorite Cullen Hightower quotes says, "Freedom without direction is chaos." So instead of simply singing along to the National Anthem or reciting the Pledge of Allegiance verbatim, I actually live my life according to principles I was taught, which are as American as the game of football.

That same dominant, competitive attitude is alive in the photography you've found in this book, from visual statements made by celebrated sports heroes, to the stories of what these legendary men - some of the NFL's all-time greatest linebackers - identify as their true calling. The league wasn't built overnight; I believe in paying homage to the guys before me, and I'm eager to reach back to them, as well as to kids coming into the game today. Photography may be on the opposite end of the spectrum from football, but there are similarities. The camera offers leadership to the photographer, even before I pick it up, look through the lens, and start snapping. I can come up with something creative, but I still have to provide comfort to people around me and bring people together to make a beautiful end result. Everybody has insecurities, but through photography, just like in the game, the goal is to walk away feeling victorious.

My mother also played a big role in my interest in photography. She urged me to take it seriously, and she also kept scrapbooks with photos of me playing football, which became motivation in a different way. In Sandersville, GA, our newspaper only came out once a week, on Mondays. I played on Friday, and waited until Monday to see if I was in the paper. She'd keep my pictures, but I used to get so mad because they'd be blurry - even the ones she shot. So I bought her a camera, then one of my own. As I learned more about shooting, I bought bigger and better cameras, and practiced whenever I found time. Looking back, I was always the guy taking and sending pictures, but I never realized it until I'd spent 11 years in the NFL. That's when I realized I liked it, and developed a sense of comfort by being able to do it well. Once, during my NFL career, I took photos during a trip to play in an international series in London. After I'd reviewed them, I'd send them to the guys in the shots. Not only did they love the photos, but they'd ask me to send more.

But let's get back to football, and how it all really started. Picture me growing up in Sandersville (a small town southwest of Augusta), in search of a physical and emotional outlet, as well as discipline, when I discovered football. I had certain gifts: natural ability, an athletic build, and a love for the game. But I also loved how football let me hit someone and get away with it, which is sort of a metaphor for how I played. I wanted to make and leave a mark on the game. And I remember the exact moment when that became clear to me.

My father knew as far back as my 8th grade year how strong my interest was to be a great football player. One day he brought home a videotape of legendary coach Lou Holtz, called *How to be a Champion*. In the videotape, I remember Lou saying before you do anything in life, there are six "musts" you've gotta do, just to have a chance to succeed -- basic guidelines. They were: Keep God first; love what you do; be committed to what you do; be honest; keep your priorities in order; and The Golden Rule - treat people the way you want to be treated. He also talked about how important it is to set goals, but don't set your goals on something you can achieve in four months; set them in a two-to-four-year time period.

That sparked my interest. I felt like, "Wow, OK. Now I have to really set my goals according to what I really wanna do." I decided that was football, and I wrote out a list. My first goal was to win a state championship ring. The second goal was to be an All-American, third was to be the best player in the state of Georgia, and fourth was to go to the Division 1 school of my choice. I took the list and taped it up on the wall beside my bed. It was the last thing I saw before I went to sleep and the first thing I saw in the morning. I fell in love with the list because I looked at it as if it was the blueprint as I was getting ready to enter 9th grade.

"I wanted to have a conscious mind to say," "No matter how bad your day went, you have another day to make it up." Or, if the day before was good, I was trying to outperform it the next day. I was learning how to compete against myself, rather than waiting on someone else to get me riled up, and that definitely came in handy, quickly. I remember the first day before spring practice began, when my high school coach said, "I have a lot of connections. I know people at Division 1 schools. If you do your part, I'll do mine to get you in." That's how he addressed the whole team. We started practice a week later, and he showed us it was all true. We had Gene Stallings from Alabama, Nebraska linebackers coach Kevin Steele, coaches from Florida State and elsewhere, coming to our small town, and I was like, "Wow...This man has credibility." I started going home and praying over that list I'd written. "Regardless of how good or bad my day goes, God, please keep me focused on what matters most. And what matters most is what's taped over my bed."

I was married to the blueprint. And if Coach told me to do something, I was trying to do extra. I felt if I did the same amount of work we were asked to do, I wouldn't stand out. So everyday I woke up focused on being better and trying to find an edge, not only among my teammates but also the opposing people. Everything I did, I'd add an extra rep. If it was three sets of five, I did three sets of six. But I was an underclassman, and Coach put his attention on the upperclassmen. He would take those guys on trips to see spring games in college: Georgia, Florida, Florida State and so on. I didn't understand that when I was younger, so I took it personally - if you leave me home, I'm not good enough. That's when I really started doing extra. I recognized that I had an opportunity to be great, so I made a commitment and stuck with it. I took all the chips and bet them on me.

Talent or not, there were obstacles. I could have gone to school playing tight end as well as linebacker, because I knew how to catch and perform. But every time Coach called a pass play, he put one of the upperclassmen in instead of me, and I took offense. Most of the time I was in a good mood, but whenever he'd come around and speak to me, I would dry-speak back to him with a direct answer, with no smile or anything behind it, like, "I'm all right." And I'd be thinking to myself, "Don't just use me to block. I know I can catch." My moment came when he called a pass play during a game, but forgot to put the upperclassman in. When I heard the play called, I expected someone was coming to take me off the field, until I realized he forgot. So we got out on the field, and I could hear him on the sidelines at the line of scrimmage, yelling at the other player, like, "Demetro, where the hell are you?!" I knew I had to catch it. The ball was snapped, it came across the middle when it was thrown and I took it for a 25-yard gain. That gave me all the confidence in the world. From that moment, everything changed. As a player, there's nothing like knowing people have confidence in your playing, especially your head coach. Everybody has a defining moment -- that was mine. Thanks, Coach Tomberlin.

Fast-forward to 1994, my senior year at Washington County High School. That was the year our high school won the state championship, I was named an All-American by *Parade* magazine and *USA Today*, as well as the Georgia High School

Football Historians Association's "Player of the Year" and "Mr. Football" by state coaches. And I was able to play at the Division 1 team of my choice - Auburn University. In two years I achieved every goal I'd set.

My shot at a career in sports had become clearer and clearer, but I still had a major hurdle to clear: the SAT. I took the test at least four times but I could never make the scores. And being the number-one player in the state of Georgia, plus the number-two linebacker in the nation, every time I took the test it was in the news, from the *Atlanta Journal-Constitution* to *USA Today*. "Hey, he's great. He's accomplished this and that, but he still has not qualified in test scores." Whenever someone mentioned me in the press, they'd put an asterisk by my name.

I remember coming home one day, wondering why it was so hard. I looked at my blueprint on the wall, and my mind went back to the 9th grade. I had to ask myself the questions: "Did I do each thing? Absolutely. And yes, I'm committed to it. I am honest. I love what I do. I treat people the way I want to be treated." Something went off in me, like, "That's all I need." And I realized, "You'll be all right. Just keep doing what you're doing." Later that night, someone asked if I'd thought about taking the ACT. I'd never heard of it, but they told me the SAT was considered more culturally biased, so I figured I might as well try. I studied my entire final year of high school. I remember taking it and still studying after the test, just in case I needed to take it again. And I remember one day during class, my mother, who was a teacher at my school, came running into the room with a sheet of paper in her hand. I'm like, "Why is my mama yelling, embarrassing me in front of everybody…?" And as she got close, I heard her say, "You passed. You can go to school."

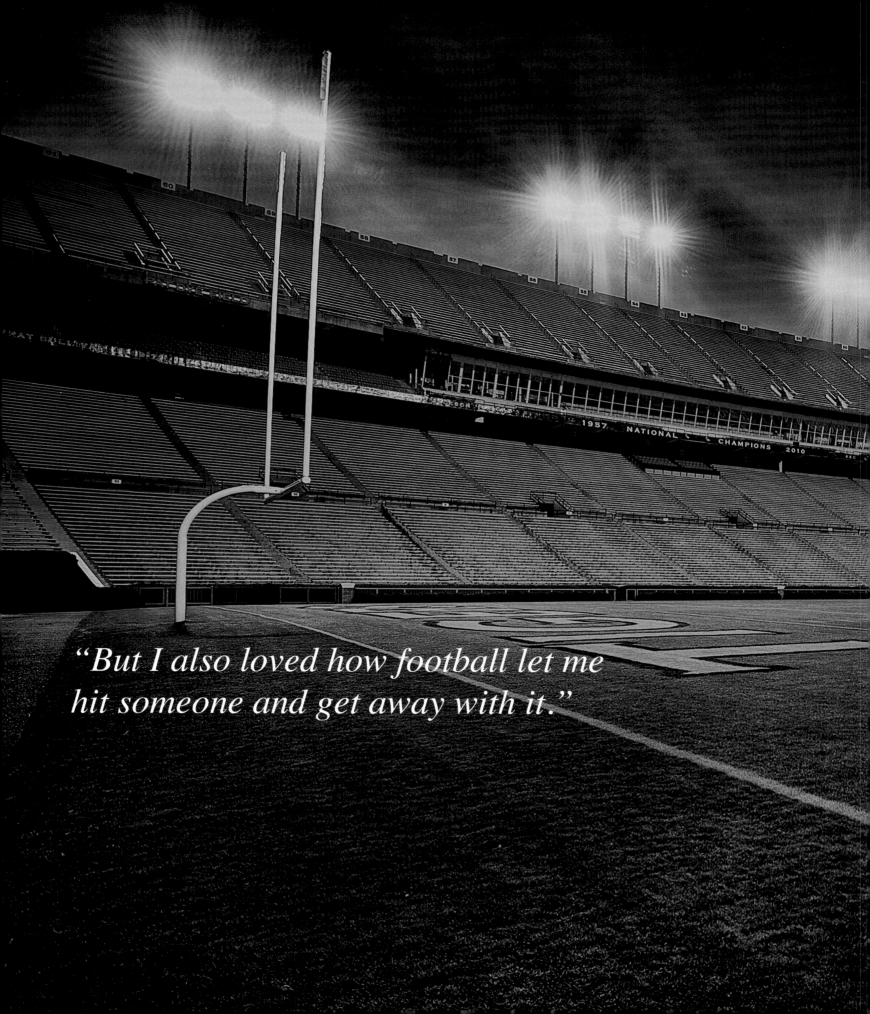

"But I also loved how football let me
hit someone and get away with it."

That was the weight of the world off my shoulders, and it really validated what I always knew. Being committed to my morals and everything on that paper - it's one thing to talk about it, but I lived it. And to see it come to fruition, that was the evidence. You can accomplish anything you want if you put your mind to it. So I did. And I took that same approach to college, and did everything I said I was going to do. I attended Auburn, and played in the 1997 SEC Championship before leaving to enter the NFL Draft. I was picked 13th overall by Cincinnati in 1998, and went on to play 15 years in the NFL, for the Bengals, the Buffalo Bills, the Philadelphia Eagles, the San Francisco 49ers and the San Diego Chargers.

I recognized at an early age I had leadership skills. I insist on excellence and I refuse to fall short of any goal without a fight. I believe there are two things we all have the ability to do: persuade and inspire. I don't want to persuade anyone, because then you're only momentarily changing a situation. I believe in inspiring change from within, because internal change is permanent. Some dream of success. Others wake up and work hard for it. These days, instead of a helmet and shoulder pads, I get suited up with a camera, multiple lenses, and various parts and pieces of equipment. I bring the same intensity to photography that I brought to the football field, and put the results on display for the world to see all over again, but in a new way. Taking my photography to this level, shooting images of legendary linebackers I greatly admire, is a way to pay respect and homage to them. I knew it was something that would take a lot of showing and proving, but I also knew when I began that I was ready. When I put my mind to something I believe in, I go the total mile.

When setting out on any successful endeavor, scrutiny and criticism just come along with the journey. I'm okay with that, because the standard in my household has always been high. With my parents' guidance, I learned to set goals for myself, and had the chance to hear them talk about morals and live their lives according to their beliefs. As a kid, it's not so much what they told me, it's what I saw them doing that stuck to my heart and showed me what moral structure is all about. So I wake up motivated, driven, looking for a challenge.

My name means "strong" and "warrior" in Japanese. And it's important for me to keep and uphold that image -- not just for America, but for my household, and for myself.

145

ACKNOWLEDGEMENTS

Publishing this book was no easy task. It truly took a community of folks to make *Behind the Mask* come to life. I am deeply appreciative to the 11 men who allowed me time and access to sit and share about their time of falling in love with the game of football and their defining moment of becoming an outlier.

To the late Chuck Bednarik and family, it was truly an honor for you guys to allow me to come into your home and get the last photography and interview session before his passing. I walked away with a wealth of knowledge that couldn't be found in any print. Derrick Brooks, I had no idea at the age of eighteen visiting Florida State University with you as my co-host that our circle would come around with you agreeing to be part of my project. You validated not only to me but the world by displaying you only need two things in life to make a change, a caring heart and time, when most people think "If I had money." Thank you Derrick. Mike Singletary, thank you for giving me confirmation on why Behind The Mask is so unique by your quote "Don't let someone else opinion become your reality." Willie Lanier, thank you for allowing me to open my mind and realize, "The world is way bigger than the block I grew up on" by understanding education is the silent legitimizer. To Kevin Greene, thank you for reminding me that we are all created equal but it is the GRIT, GRIND, and COMMITMENT that propels you to Hall of Fame Status.

Rickey Jackson, thank you for finally picking up the phone so we could put an itinerary together instead of winging it, LOL. Your gift of Rickey Jackson seasonings are top-notch in the Spikes household. Bobby Bell, thank you for my constant reminder that young people to reinvent themselves and make constant adjustments to become better. Ted Hendricks, thank you for reminding me there is a difference between being injured and hurt, but pain is controllable. Harry Carson, thank you for your candid vivid, story on growing up in the south during the civil rights era. It reminds me every day of my duty to continue to be that example to all young kids from rural towns like Sandersville, GA. London Fletcher, thank you for sharing your story of trials and tribulations with the world. Your story is living proof that a piece of coal has to go through friction in order to become a diamond. Cornelius Bennett, thank you for allowing me to share your most intimate thoughts about the game you dearly love even though you're not excited about the attention that comes from the media, LOL. You deserve to be in the Hall of Fame and you will…I'm claiming it!

Thank you, Bill Polian and Dick LeBeau for lending your Hall of Fame eye. To my videographer Rico, thank you for your flexible hours and creative mind. To my creative designer D. L. Warfield, thank you for bringing out my artistic side so that the world can appreciate another layer to me. Dawn Michelle Hardy, thank you for giving me insight as my project manager when no one else saw the passion and uniqueness of *Behind The Mask*. Mike B. Jordan, thank you for getting all of the stories out of my head and sharing with the world. To Mike Moreland, thank you for the first lesson you gave me on my camera. That lesson and you serving as my mentor took *Behind The Mask* from a thought and made it reality. Carmin Romanelli and Ashyln Barefoot at Getty Images and to Joshua Blair and John Gilmore of Brandthumb, thank you all for supporting *Behind The Mask* as you have. Thank you Linda Babl for being my contributing editor for Ted Hendricks. Thank you Kia Stone for the brainstorming session when I was contemplating retiring from the NFL. Blame this book on the last cold adult beverage you ordered.